EARLY CHILDHOOD EDUCATION SERIES
Leslie R. Williams, Editor
Millie Almy, Senior Advisor

ADVISORY BOARD: Barbara T. Bowman, Harriet K. Cuffaro, Stephanie Feeney, Doris Pronin Fromberg, Celia Genishi, Dominic F. Gullo, Alice Sterling Honig, Elizabeth Jones, Gwen Morgan, David Weikert

(Continued)

Understanding Assessment and Evaluation in Early Childhood Education

Dominic F. Gullo

Teachers College, Columbia University
New York and London

Published by Teachers College Press, 1234 Amsterdam Avenue, New York, N.Y. 10027

Library of Congress Cataloging-in-Publication Data

Gullo, Dominic F.
    Understanding assessment and evaluation in early childhood
education / Dominic F. Gullo
        p. cm. — (Early childhood education series)
    Includes bibliographical references and index.
    ISBN 0-8077-3308-3 (paper). — ISBN 0-8077-3309-1 (cloth)
    1. Educational tests and measurements—United States. 2. Early
childhood education—United States—Evaluation. I. Title. II. Series.
LB3051.G85 1994
372.12'64'0973—dc20   93-29495

ISBN: 0-8077-3309-1
ISBN: 0-8077-3308-3 (paper)

Printed on acid-free paper
Manufactured in the United States of America
99 98 97 96 95 94 93   8 7 6 5 4 3 2 1

CONTENTS

Understanding the role of assessment and evaluation in early child-hood education is a complex process. There are vast numbers of children in early childhood programs who could be affected by assessment and evaluation. Whether the effect is positive or negative could ultimately be determined by the early childhood teacher's understanding of the process. Understanding the process of assessment and evaluation in early childhood involves understanding when and how to use assessment and evaluation; understanding how the child's development affects the process; and understanding the relationship between assessment, evaluation, and a curriculum that is developmentally appropriate for the child. Some of the understanding is common sense. Some of the understanding requires formal and deliberate learning on the part of the early childhood professional. Some of the understanding requires going beyond conventional wisdom and good intentions, for good intentions and conventional wisdom may lead to inappropriate practices.

The following anecdote about a grandfather visiting his grandson's prekindergarten classroom illustrates that point. It will also serve as a framework to reflect on while reading the rest of the book.

> I recently took my grandson to be tested for admission to the 4-year-old kindergarten. His test consisted of recognizing a few shapes and some colors. As a faithful viewer of Sesame Street, he was able to correctly identify the colors and shapes on the test. Hurrah! Nick was fully admitted to 4-year-old kindergarten.
>
> As a wife and working mother, my daughter was elated to have Nick out of day care and into a suburban school system of high repute. She warned me, "Dad, you can pick Nick up after school, but don't screw this up! Just keep your mouth shut! Call

for him, don't talk to anyone, and bring him straight home!" I promised to pick Nick up faithfully and not cause trouble.

After Nick had been attending school for a few weeks, I called for him one day and bumped into his teacher. Introducing myself to the teacher as a retired tie salesman, I asked her why she had admitted my grandson. The teacher replied that he had passed the screening test. I then asked her what would have happened if he confused blue and green, or if he hadn't known the difference between a square and a circle. Would he have been admitted? "No," replied the teacher, "in that case he would have failed the screening, and we would not have admitted him." I then asked the teacher if my grandson was definitely admitted and would not be kicked out on the basis of my silly questions. (My daughter's warnings were still ringing in my ears.)

After the teacher reassured me that my "very bright" grandson would not be expelled because of any question I might ask, I asked the following question: "Wouldn't it make more sense to admit the children who don't know their shapes and colors and teach them these things rather than admit the children who already know all these things?" The teacher looked at me like left-over mashed potatoes. I was obviously a troublesome, ignorant old man. She explained that when she took her master's degree in early childhood she studied both the theory and research of readiness. "Readiness," she announced, "is a concept that helps educators determine who is ready to benefit from school instruction and who is still too immature."

"Oh," I replied, "I would have thought all 4-year-olds are 'immature.'"

Again she looked at me in that sad, tired way people do when they speak to the hopelessly stupid. She went on to explain, at some length, that maturity was determined by the year-by-year progression of normal children through the required stages of child development. I also heard how expert psychometricians had scientifically developed this entrance exam and that based on a normal distribution of 4-year-old children, my grandson was definitely in the top half and "ready" to benefit from 4-year-old kindergarten at this point.

I thanked the teacher for her patience and careful explanation, but couldn't keep myself from asking just one more question. "Next year my grandson, who is already testing in your top half, will have had the added benefit of being in your 4-year-old kindergarten for a whole year. Won't he learn a lot more and be even further ahead of the 4-year-old who failed your admission exam and who spent this year at home or someplace else without the benefit of your kindergarten? Will the 4-year-old rejects ever catch up?"

This time the teacher looked at me as if my comment called for a two-fisted reply, but she was counting to ten. I beat a hasty retreat without waiting for her explanation. The message she had delivered was quite clear. I've heard similar gobbledygook many times from test makers, administrators, and teachers. What she was saying quite directly without using the exact words ought to be emblazoned over every public kindergarten in America: *The children we teach best are those who need us least.**

---

*This personal communication was provided by Martin Haberman, who by his own admission is a grandfather, although not actually a retired tie salesman. Martin is, however, Professor of Education at the University of Wisconsin at Milwaukee.

ACKNOWLEDGMENTS

My most sincere gratitude goes to Doris Fromberg and Leslie Williams who encouraged me to undertake this project. Without their encouragement, I would not have taken the opportunity to consolidate my thoughts and clarify my ideas.

Thanks are due to Susan Liddicoat whose gentle nature and subtle nudging kept me on task. Thanks also goes to Susan for her helpful suggestions for revisions.

Thank you Milwaukee Public Schools and particularly Garfield Elementary School for being innovative as well as permitting me to be a first-hand player in school reform. The young children of Milwaukee and their families also thank you.

Special thanks to Nick Anastasiow, mentor, colleague, and friend.

To Matt and Tim (T.J.), who taught me through the years that we shouldn't always believe what we see and that children are the most accurate reflectors of life.

To Jeanne, my partner, who makes those with whom she comes in contact, recognize their potential and ultimately reach it.

Part I

**Introducing Assessment
and Evaluation in
Early Childhood Education**

CHAPTER 1

Assessment and Evaluation in the Early Childhood Years

A child is born! Within the first 60 seconds of life it is determined that the newborn has a heart rate of 120 beats per minute, she entered the outside world crying vigorously and breathing regularly, she withdrew her arms and legs when touched, she vehemently rejected the efforts of others to straighten her limbs, and her skin seemed to glow from the top of her head to the tip of her toes. Her score—10.

From the moment of birth, assessment and evaluation play an important part in our lives. The illustration above is an often repeated scene in hospital delivery rooms throughout the United States today. During the first minute of life, infants are observed, assessed, and their Apgar score is determined. Five minutes later, another Apgar score is established. The Apgar Scale (Apgar, 1953) is a widely used assessment instrument that determines the newborn's physical well-being. Scores can range from zero to ten with a high score indicating good physical condition. The score provides a quick and valid indication of the need for possible and/or immediate intervention in the areas of respiration, circulation, pulmonary functioning, and other sensorimotor functions.

In 1904, the French Minister of Education recognized the need for a classification system to assist educators in admitting, placing, and developing educational programs for children entering special schools. As a result, a special commission was appointed in Paris to study the situation. A psychologist, by the name of Alfred Binet, was a member of this commission. By 1905, the Binet Scale was developed and used as an educational placement instrument by French schools (Kelley & Surbeck, 1983). The educational testing movement had begun!

The Binet Scale and the Apgar Scale demonstrate two aspects of assessment and evaluation in early childhood. Assessment and evaluation have been around for a long time, and they begin early in the lifetime of an individual.

Recently, in the field of early childhood education, there has been an ongoing debate related to the various roles assessment and evaluation play within the profession. This debate has focused on what types of assessment and evaluation are appropriate for young children and what uses and misuses can result from the outcomes of these evaluations. Most of this debate has focused specifically on the misuses of standardized testing in early childhood education (see, for example, Worthen & Spandel, 1991).

Meisels (1987, 1989a) contends that standardized test results are often misused and may lead to undesirable effects on both children and the curriculum. Some of the ways in which misuses of standardized test results affect children are

1. Prohibiting children from entering a program due to their test performance even though they are of legal entrance age.
2. Placing children in inappropriate ability groups.
3. Using children's test performance on developmental screening to predict their future academic performance.

Regarding the early childhood curriculum, Meisels (1989a) maintains that standardized tests may narrow the scope of the curriculum if teachers teach to the test so that their students' scores are increased. In addition, schools may look to tests to determine curricular goals and objectives, thereby relinquishing their duties of curriculum development to the test writers and publishers.

While much of the current focus in the debate is on standardized testing issues, it is important to look beyond. The process of assessment and evaluation is more than simply testing and measuring. Understanding children's performances or academic or behavioral competencies involves more than looking at their test scores. It is more than comparing one child's scores to those of other children in the same grade or developmental level. It is what underlies those scores that is important to know. That is, what may have influenced the child's performance and resulted in a particular score on a particular test. This is especially true in early childhood education due to the qualitative differences in children's thinking at this stage as compared with later stages of development.

What is essential is that professionals who work with young children *understand* the constructs underlying assessment and evaluation in early childhood so they can make appropriate decisions regarding the selection of assessment instruments and methods. And, given the results of assessment procedures, to make informed and appropriate decisions about children and curriculum. The issues surrounding testing and measurement in early childhood have become complex. Appropriate use (or misuse) of assessment and/or evaluation information, can influence the direction of an individual child's or group of children's early as well as later education and developmental trajectories. This book's purpose is to help early childhood practitioners to develop the essential understanding they require and to illuminate many of the issues involved in assessment and evaluation.

THEMES GUIDING THE DISCUSSION OF THE BOOK

In this book, three themes will emerge and guide the discussion of understanding assessment and evaluation in early childhood. These themes will provide the underlying conceptual framework, both theoretical and philosophical, for the topics presented.

Development and Evaluation

First and foremost, the central theme will focus on the consideration of the child's developmental stage and characteristics, and how these factors relate to assessment and evaluation procedures and outcomes. The focal question here is, how does one use assessment to formulate appropriate questions that will elicit appropriate answers? The premise of this question is that assessment is a means of determining what the child knows, what the child can and cannot do, what knowledge or information the child has acquired as a result of a particular experience, to what degree the child can appropriately use the information he or she has acquired, and so on. In order to ask the right kinds of questions to determine these things, educators have to be able to match words, situations, pictures, activities, objects, gestures, and other types of stimuli to what children, given their stage of development, can meaningfully process. If such a match exists, one can expect that the response given by the child will reflect such understanding. If the match does not exist, then the response may not reflect the child's actual level of competence in the particular area being assessed.

Effects of Assessment and Evaluation on Children

Another important theme that will be central to many of the discussions in this book is the effects that assessment and evaluation have on the child. In part this is a validity and reliability issue. That is, how *exactly* is what is being assessed being *accurately* assessed. The question lies not so much in the psychometric properties of the assessment or evaluation instrument (e.g., reliability and validity)—assessment and evaluation need not even involve instrumentation—but rather in the validity of the process being undertaken to make certain decisions.

Again, it is necessary to return to a developmental principle. A fundamental premise of stage theories in child development is that while all children proceed through the same stages of development in the same sequence, not all children proceed at the same rate. This is particularly noted in the area of cognitive development, an aspect of child development often assessed in early childhood education. Another aspect of this type of developmental sequence and rate is that by the time all typically developing children reach the age of 8, many of the individual differences observed earlier, related to rate of biological maturation, have evened themselves out (Anastasiow, 1986; Gullo, 1992).

If we evaluate children and use this information as an indication of their future academic potential or use it inappropriately to group children into homogeneous ability groups, the differences that will result in children's academic environment as a result of these evaluations could be dramatic. When given labels, primarily the result of assessment findings that are invalid for these purposes, most children will perform accordingly. In the case of homogeneous ability groups, the experiences that children have, or don't have, in the "lower" groups will inhibit them from "moving up" to the "higher" ability groups. This is true even when children's later developmental levels indicate that they could have met the behavioral expectations of the latter group. In this manner, evaluation affects children.

Relationship Between Curriculum and Evaluation

Broadly speaking, the early education curriculum can be defined as a set of experiences that can occur in almost any setting that children happen to be engaged in activity. It is not limited to a "classroom" in the formal sense of the word. The curriculum experience includes the physical setting, the materials, the specific content, as well as social and physical interaction. Another assessment and evaluation validity issue that is integrated throughout this book is the importance of the match between what is being assessed and what is occurring within the curriculum. Within this issue, two topics must be considered, both concerned with the relationship between curriculum and evaluation. First, relationship refers to the parallel structure that should exist between what is being evaluated and what is being presented vis-a-vis the curriculum. In order to be valid, there should be a close match between the curriculum and evaluation instrumentation. Curriculum here refers to both content as well as methods. A second topic that will be considered regarding curriculum and evaluation relationship has to do with influence. The questions that will be discussed are: Should curriculum influence what evaluation techniques and materials will be used?; or Should the evaluation influence what and how the content of the curriculum should be taught?

Curriculum and Evaluation Comparability. Although an individual is assessed to determine academic and/or curricular performance or competence, the process of individual assessment occurs within the context of the curriculum. As such, the specific evaluation or assessment content and procedure should reflect the curricular content and instructional strategies that are being utilized. If the curriculum is implemented using one set of assumptions and evaluated using others, children's performance may not reflect what they have actually attained as a result of participating in the curriculum. This is especially true for young children, who by their developmental nature have a difficult time generalizing knowledge and performance from one context to other contexts.

A good example of this is the correlation, or lack of it, between how reading and math are taught in early childhood education, and how reading and math performance is evaluated. The teaching of reading and math generally focuses on process rather than on the attainment of isolated skills. The "whole-language" approach to reading/language/writing and the "manipulative-math" approach to arithmetic are good examples of process-oriented teaching strategies. In both of these instructional strategies, it is not the "right" answer that is the focus of instruction, but rather the problem-solving strategies that are used to reach the answers. Both approaches emphasize using divergent problem-solving strategies, multiple "probable" responses, and individualized timetables for reaching mastery.

But a problematic, and critical, consequence has arisen from process-oriented early education curricula in that it may be difficult to reliably evaluate the processes involved in these types of instructional strategies. Because of this, many schools are relying on "traditional" assessment instruments and evaluation techniques that are usually product oriented with an emphasis on the right answer. In addition, an implicit assumption is that all children being assessed should be at the same place at the same time. Often the outcome is that evaluation findings do not accurately reflect children's actual competence resulting from curricular experiences. This may precipitate a misconception that the curriculum is not effective or that the children are not competent in acquiring the curricular content.

Evaluation and Curriculum—An Influential Relationship. A question that seems to be part of every inquiry, scientific and nonscientific, is, which came first? This question is appropriate here. It is important to remember that evaluation should be used as a tool to measure and determine any number of attributes relative to the individual or the curriculum. As such, one should be cognizant of the characteristics of the curriculum in selecting assessment procedures. Evaluation should not determine curriculum content or strategies. Rather, curriculum should determine which type of assessment instruments and strategies should be used.

Implications. The two topics discussed above, about the relationship between evaluation and curriculum, overlap but exert their influence in different ways. The first one, related to comparability, influences what teachers may believe about children's competence. If the assessment materials or procedures are not comparable to the curriculum and a student's score is low, the teacher may believe that the student is not doing well. The second topic, related to influence, may affect the curriculum content or instructional strategies. If children do not do well on assessment instruments that are not well matched to what is being taught or how the content is delivered, teachers may be inclined to "reconstruct" the curriculum so that there is a closer match, rather than maintaining the curriculum and instead considering selecting a new method of assessment or evaluation.

These three themes—the relationship between evaluation and child development, the effects of assessment and evaluation on children, and the relationship between curriculum and evaluation—will be apparent throughout this book, although they will not necessarily be reiterated explicitly in each chapter.

PARAMETERS OF EARLY CHILDHOOD

In order to establish a common frame of reference regarding the period of development referred to as early childhood, it is necessary to define its use in this book. Early childhood can be described from three different but related perspectives: chronological age; developmentally; or in the traditional school setting, by grade level.

Chronologically, early childhood is defined as those ages between birth and 8 years old. These are the years of greatest dependency on others and according to some (Scarr, 1976) the period of greatest biological similarity with respect to the course of development, particularly cognitive development. In addition to recognizing that this age span consists of many universal developmental traits, it has also been recognized as being uniquely different than those ages beyond the 8th year. There is, in fact, a biophysical change in the brain that occurs at around age 7 or 8 (Anastasiow, 1986). The maturation and resulting integration of particular brain functions at this age make it possible for children to learn things at age 7 or 8 that were not possible at age 5.

The developmental definition of early childhood is understandably very closely related to the chronological definition. According to Piaget (1963), a developmental child psychologist whose work has significantly influenced and shaped the field of early childhood education, the parameters of early childhood are captured by the sensorimotor and preoperational periods of cognitive development. These two stages of cognitive development include approximately the first 8 years of life and are characterized by the unique manner that children use to process information, construct knowledge, and solve problems. As a result, children in this developmental period require specialized instruction and learning environments.

Differences between the chronological and developmental definitions of early childhood are best illustrated by children whose developmental timetables are either accelerated or delayed. Children who are chronologically beyond the early childhood years, but whose cognitive development is within the preoperational stage, do better when taught with techniques and materials appropriate for early childhood education. Conversely, some early childhood education strategies may not be appropriate for children beyond preoperations, but whose age falls within the defined early childhood years.

Finally, early childhood can be defined by grade level (National Association of State Boards of Education; NASBE, 1988). This is particularly appropriate in the school setting. Early childhood education covers those grade levels between prekindergarten and third grade. Increasingly, more and more schools are including prekindergarten as part of their regular academic programs. These programs generally start at age 4, however, some may begin as early as 3 years old.

Early childhood education generally refers to programs appropriate for children ages birth to 8 years old. These programs may be housed in various locations, ranging from private facilities (e.g., child care centers, nursery schools, hospitals) to agencies (e.g., Head Start), to public school programs.

ASSESSMENT AND EVALUATION: DEFINING THE TERMS

In order to continue the discussion of assessment and evaluation in early childhood, it is important to define some general terminology used throughout the book. The terms and concepts defined here will not be related to specific assessment or evaluation techniques, as these will be defined later in an appropriate context. Rather, the terminology presented here represents concepts that are pertinent across the wide array of issues related to assessment and evaluation.

Assessment

Assessment is a procedure used to determine the degree to which an individual child possesses a certain attribute. The term *assessment* can be used interchangeably with measurement. According to Boehm (1992), there are several purposes for assessment in early childhood.

One purpose for assessment is to gain an understanding of a child's overall development. An understanding of the child's development would be helpful for the teacher in order to identify those areas where specific help or teaching is required. Identifying emerging areas of development and pinpointing those areas already possessed would provide information useful in determining a child's readiness for instruction and aid in identifying the appropriate forms and levels of classroom instruction.

A second purpose for assessing an individual child is for the teacher to gain a better understanding of how the child is progressing within the program. In doing so, teachers can advance their knowledge concerning the diverse learning styles and strategies used by various children. In addition, the collective assessments of children's academic achievement can be used to measure the effectiveness of programs and interventions.

A final reason for assessing individual children is to identify those who are at risk for academic failure or are potentially in need of special education services. Such assessment procedures may begin as screening and lead to further in-depth evaluation or diagnosis. Included here may also be the evaluation of environmental factors that influence both learning and development.

Academic readiness tests, developmental screening tests, and diagnostic tests are all types of formal assessments. As will be seen, information from individual assessments may be combined in education evaluation procedures.

Evaluation

Evaluation is the process of making judgments about the merit, value, or worth of educational programs, projects, materials, or techniques.

Assessments may be used during the process of educational evaluation in order to make these judgments. Evaluation often includes "research-like" techniques in order to carry out the plan. According to Smith and Glass (1987), the judgments and conclusions derived from evaluation are based upon evidence. Evidence can include both systematic as well as unsystematic observations of program outcomes.

Evaluations can either be comparative or noncomparative, according to Smith and Glass. In a comparative evaluation, alternative programs' outcomes are assessed and compared. In a study by Gullo, Bersani, Clements, and Bayless (1986), for example, kindergarten programs using either a half-day, full-day, or alternate full-day schedule were compared to determined their relative effects on children's academic achievement and classroom social behavior. The relative benefits of alternative programs can be assessed by comparative evaluation techniques, and decisions made regarding programs based upon empirical evidence.

In noncomparative evaluation, program outcomes are assessed in one group only, and these results are compared with an absolute criterion (Smith & Glass, 1987). For example, Head Start programs are evaluated annually using the "Head Start Program Performance Standards Self-Assessment/Validation Instrument" (SAVI, U.S. Department of Health and Human Services, 1979). The SAVI includes criteria for meeting program standards for each of the components in the Head Start Program. Reasons for program noncompliance are provided for each program criterion. For each area of the program not in compliance with the standards, a strategy for meeting criteria must be developed.

Similarly, the National Association for the Education of Young Children (NAEYC)(1985) has established the National Academy of Early Childhood Programs. This is an evaluation approach based upon criterion standards used for accrediting early childhood programs. In this evaluation, different components of an early childhood program are compared with standards developed by NAEYC. Accreditation by this organization has become a nationally recognized standard of quality.

Alternative Assessment

Alternative assessment refers to an assessment option that focuses on methods other than strict adherence to the standard tests and measurement paradigm. Authentic assessment (Chittenden, 1991) and portfolio assessment (Shanklin & Conrad, 1991) are terms sometimes used interchangeably with alternative assessment. According to Chittenden (1991), although nomenclature varies, the goals of alternative assessment appear to be consistent. The first goal of alternative assessment is to incorporate actual classroom work into individual assessment. Secondly, a critical goal of alternative assessment procedures is to enhance both children's and teachers' participation in the assessment process. Finally, alternative assessment attempts to meet some of the accountability concerns of school districts and funding agencies.

OVERVIEW OF THE CHAPTERS

Now that a common frame of reference has been established regarding terminology and early childhood development and education, and the general focus of the book has been described, it may be helpful to have a brief overview of the remaining chapters. The book is divided structurally into three parts.

In Part I, issues concerned with the unique relationship between the field of early childhood and assessment and evaluation will be introduced and discussed. Chapter 2 discusses issues related to the role of assessment and evaluation in early childhood. Topics include specific purposes of evaluation and assessment in early education and the manner in which evaluation and assessment are processes, integrated into the curriculum and instruction of early childhood programs. Development is the primary topic of Chapter 3. Developmental characteristics of children are described, along with the ways these characteristics may affect children's test-taking behaviors.

Part II of the book focuses on formal assessment and evaluation in early childhood education, and includes three chapters. Chapter 4 describes the various types of standardized instruments that are appropriate for use in early childhood. The reader will become aware of the different types of results (scores) that can be generated by various types of assessment and evaluation procedures. Interpretation of the outcomes as well as the appropriate uses of the results are discussed. Psychometric characteristics of tests are also presented. The particular importance of validity, reliability, and practicality for early education are explained. Chapter 5 discusses how testing may have negative impact on children, curriculum, and professional trends. Suggestions for overcoming these shortcomings are presented.

Chapter 6 focuses on one specific issue that had been presented briefly in the previous chapter: the potential influence of testing on one's interpretation of school readiness. This chapter focuses on the ways testing has been misused in determining children's readiness for school as well as the practices that accompany this process.

The main focus of the three chapters in Part III is informal assessment and evaluation procedures in early childhood education. In chapter 7 various types of informal assessment and evaluation procedures appropriate for use in early childhood settings are described, and their advantages and disadvantages discussed. Topics in chapter 8 include defining alternative assessment, types of alternative assessment, and strategies for developing an alternative assessment program. In chapter 9, ways to incorporate alternative assessment into the various early childhood curricular areas are described.

In appendix A, a glossary of assessment instruments used in early childhood education is presented. Instruments are categorized into developmental screening instruments, readinesss and/or achievement tests, and diagnostic tests.

In appendix B, a case study of one school's journey through the evaluation and assessment planning process is detailed. The questions they asked, the solutions they arrived at, and the products they developed are presented.

CHAPTER 2

Putting Early Childhood Assessment and Evaluation in Perspective

As stated in chapter 1, the process of evaluation constitutes more than simply testing and measuring. In most test and measurement textbooks, general psychometric properties of tests and measurements are discussed and readers are cautioned to take these characteristics into consideration when making decisions about which measurements to use for what purposes and in what situations. These characteristics are to be considered in the construction of teacher-made tests as well. While these considerations are important and can be generally applied to most students in educational settings, early childhood education presents a somewhat different scenario.

During most of the early childhood years, it is difficult to measure and assess bits of knowledge and skills that are isolated from other types of knowledge and skills. Young children are not reliable test takers due to the many different confining personal, developmental, and environmental factors that affect their behaviors (this notion will be expanded upon in Chapter 3). In addition, just as children do not develop in an isolated manner, they do not acquire knowledge nor learn specific bits of information or skills without learning other things within the contextual framework. As a result, measuring whether children have acquired specific information may be a somewhat difficult, invalid, and unreliable task if teachers view the assessment and evaluation process as being a similar one across the various age, developmental, and grade levels.

Another difficulty arises out of the situation that is prevalent in many discussions of tests and measurements; it is assumed that the test taker is a reader. This is understandably not the case for most of the children in early education settings. Therefore, alternative means of assessing children must be used. However, alternative procedures and materials come with their own problems. Questions related to reliability, validity, predictability, and generalizabilty are often raised. In addition, comparability problems surface.

In this chapter, two facets of assessment and evaluation in early childhood education will be discussed: the purposes for assessment and evaluation in early childhood education; and viewing assessment and evaluation as part of the educative process.

PURPOSES FOR ASSESSMENT AND EVALUATION
IN EARLY CHILDHOOD EDUCATION

Many people equate standardized testing with assessment and evaluation. As such, standardized tests are generally applied at the end of an educational experience and used for many purposes—some appropriate, some inappropriate. Teachers often fear testing because it implies that they are the ones being evaluated. While schools should be held accountable for learning, using assessment and evaluation findings as a means of determining whether one teacher is teaching better than another is not an appropriate use of evaluation results. While teacher accountability and appropriate use of evaluation can be compatible, the information gleaned from individual assessment and program evaluation should be used to reflect and inform the educative process rather than to force it into arbitrary quality categories.

As stated earlier, evaluation is more than simply standardized testing, and there are numerous reasons for assessing children and evaluating programs. As will be seen, each of these purposes are related. In all, four general purposes for assessment and evaluation will be discussed in this chapter. The first two deal specifically with assessing the individual child, and the last two deal with evaluating program effectiveness.

Individual Assessment

The first purpose of assessment and evaluation in early childhood education settings is to *determine the child's current level of aca-*

demic and/or developmental functioning. Individual assessment is crucial to determine the starting point from which to begin the curriculum process with children. Typically two aspects are considered within this framework.

The first is the usefulness of determining what type of academic skills and factual knowledge the child has. Academic skills are the types of knowledge and problem solving abilities children have as a direct result of experiencing curriculum activities. Academic skills are needed to continue or progress through the curriculum sequence. These include such things as knowledge of number, conceptual knowledge, logical knowledge, factual knowledge, and so on. According to Meisels (1987), readiness tests might be one useful tool in determining the child's current level of academic functioning, and he maintains that readiness tests can be used to assist teachers in planning the curriculum. In addition, information from readiness tests can help teachers determine how prepared children are to engage in particular curricular activities and therefore whether they can benefit from them. While readiness tests can be a useful tool in determining children's relative academic functioning and preparedness, cautions accompany their use. These will be discussed in chapter 4.

Readiness tests provide one means of determining children's academic functioning; However, there are other less formal means. Observing children engaged in activities is very useful in determining their level of functioning within academic settings. Talking with them and asking questions is another. Cryan (1986) lists a number of informal techniques of assessing academic readiness in children. In addition to direct observation, he includes interviews, checklists, samples of children's work, and anecdotal records. Used systematically, such methods will provide the teacher with much useful information. These are described in chapter 7.

The second aspect of assessing children is to determine their current level of developmental functioning. Knowledge about children's motor development, language development, or cognitive development is essential to enable teachers to design appropriate curriculum activities. Another reason to ascertain children's current level of developmental functioning is to determine whether they might benefit from alternative curricular experiences. A developmental screening test may help provide this information. According to Meisels (1987, 1989b), developmental screening tests can be used to help identify those children who may need further diagnostic testing to determine whether they require intervention or special education services. Further, Meisels indicates that by identifying children's levels of developmental functioning, teachers may better understand those children who are in need of a modified or individualized curriculum. Again, there are cautions in administering, interpreting, and applying the results from these instruments, as will be discussed in chapter 4.

The second purpose of assessment and/or evaluation in early education settings is to determine what knowledge or skills children have acquired as a result of specific experiences in the early education setting. This type of evaluation is useful to teachers in ascertaining if specific educational goals and objectives are being met and how children's skills and knowledge have changed as a result of a specific curriculum experience.

For example, a field trip to a farm during a unit on animals may result in children having a better understanding of which animals live on farms and which animals live in zoos, and what baby animals belong to which adult animals or what food or other products come from which animals. To determine this, teachers should probably discuss these aspects of farm animals in an informal manner to learn what information children have a good, a limited, or no, grasp of. This will help the teacher structure the field trip. Then, following the trip, a similar evaluation process, a kind of debriefing, should take place. The teacher can then determine what the children have acquired from their experience on the farm. This kind of information can be used by teachers to develop further activities for the whole class or individual children and so achieve their curriculum objectives.

Similar evaluations should be made about all types of classroom activities, both formal (specific lessons on specific information) as well as informal (free choice activities). They will provide useful information to the early childhood classroom teacher.

Program Evaluation

A third purpose for evaluation and/or assessment is to determine the effectiveness of an educational experience while it is in progress. Evaluation with this purpose is often referred to as formative evaluation. Formative evaluation refers to assessments of quality that are focused on curricular programs that may still be modified. Following a program's design and implementation, formative evaluation is undertaken to assess the program's progress as well as to provide information that could lead to the program's improvement (Royce, Murray, Lazar, & Darlington, 1982). The major purpose of formative evaluation is to determine whether or not the curricular goals and objectives are being met.

According to Wortham (1990), many different aspects of the early education experience can be monitored through formative evaluation. These include equipment and materials used to implement the curriculum, specific curriculum activities, as well as teachers' behaviors during the implementation process. At the heart of the formative evaluation strategy is the gathering of evidence regarding the efficacy of the various components of the curricular and instruction sequences, and the consideration of this evidence in order to isolate the probable deficits and to suggest possible modifications. The specific strategies used during formative evaluation in early education settings may be of a formal or informal nature.

Specific instruments have been designed to evaluate different components of the early education program. Louise Derman-Sparks (1989), for example, has developed strategies for identifying bias in early childhood programs. In her book, she identifies different types of bias and the ways in which bias can occur in early education settings. She discusses racial bias, cultural bias, gender bias, as well as stereotyping in general. Derman-Sparks elaborates on how bias can occur within the environment, materials, books, and activities found in the early childhood program. She also discusses ways the curriculum can be evaluated for bias and provides strategies for modifying the curriculum to eliminate it.

Schweinhart (1988) provides administrators with a means of evaluating whether the administrative characteristics of their programs indicate good early childhood programming. He discusses a number of administrative concerns including enrollment limit setting, teacher-child ratios, staff training, supervisory support and inservice training, as well as the importance of family needs and involvement in the program.

The early childhood environment can be evaluated and monitored using an instrument designed by Harms and Clifford (1980). The Early Childhood Environment Rating Scale, which can be used by classroom teachers to assess children's personal care routines, furnishings and displays for children, language reasoning experiences, fine and gross motor activities, creative activities, social development activities, and adult needs. Each of the factors in the environment are rated on a scale from 1 (inadequate) to 7 (excellent). At rating points 1, 3, 5, and 7, a description of the characteristics for the factor at that rating point is given. Suggestions are given for modifications if the factors are not rated satisfactorily.

As can be seen, the primary goal of formative evaluation is to modify the program to enhance it. Formative evaluation should take place on a continuing basis during the implementation life of the program, rather than at the end of the program when modifications would not be beneficial to those completing the program.

The final purpose of evaluation is determining the effectiveness of an educational experience at its conclusion. Evaluation of this nature is called summative evaluation. In summative evaluation, information is gathered regarding the worth of an overall instructional sequence so that decisions can be made regarding whether to retain or adopt that sequence. This sequence can either be a specific one (e.g., whole language reading instruction or basal reading instructional approach) or one that represents a whole program approach (e.g., full-day kindergarten or half-day kindergarten schedule).

Take, for example, the question of deciding between a half-day or full-day kindergarten schedule—a dilemma that many school districts are facing. Obviously there are advantages and disadvantages to both. In a summative evaluation, the evaluator would be interested in determining if the benefits of a full-day kindergarten schedule warrant either keeping a full-day schedule or changing to it from the more traditional half-day schedule. At the end of the school year, the summative evaluation might investigate what effects the full-day kindergarten schedule (as compared with the half-day kindergarten schedule) has on a number of variables: end of the year general achievement levels, reading levels, depth of curriculum coverage, parent satisfaction, child attitudes toward school and learning, teacher satisfaction, retention, attendance, social development, ease of transition into first grade, and so forth. With this kind of information, the task of deciding whether to retain or adopt the full-day kindergarten schedule is made easier, and the decision would be based on more objective evidence.

In summative evaluation, the end of an educational sequence is somewhat arbitrary. For example, in making the decision of whether to adopt a full-day kindergarten schedule, the end of the instruction sequence could be put at the end of the kindergarten year or it could be put at the end of third grade, which is often identified as the end of early education (Bredekamp, 1987; Gullo, 1992). An evaluator might decide on the latter if it is anticipated that some of the effects of the full-day kindergarten may not reveal themselves until later in the child's educational experience.

Another example of when defining the end of the curriculum at different times might be appropriate would be in assessing the relative benefits of using a "whole language" approach to reading. While whole language strategies are used widely in prekindergarten and kindergarten, the rate that children develop and demonstrate various reading skills under this system may differ from those children who focus on the specific and isolated reading skills that are emphasized more in a basal approach to reading instruction. Therefore, the end of kindergarten or first grade may not be the appropriate time to evaluate this approach and compare it with children instructed using the reading skills approach. While children using the whole language approach will eventually consolidate these skills, it may not be until the end of second grade or the beginning of third grade that a valid appraisal of the child's reading ability can be obtained using traditional reading assessment instruments.

While summative evaluation is important in making curricular decisions, one must make the appropriate determination of when it should occur. Formative and summative evaluation should go hand-in-hand. Formative evaluation offers information on how curriculum could or should be modified to make it more efficacious, while summative evaluation elucidates the overall effectiveness of the experience.

EVALUATION AS PART OF THE EDUCATIVE PROCESS

It should be evident from the above discussion, which delineates the various reasons for assessment and evaluation in early childhood education, that assessment and evaluation are a large part of the process of educating the child. Assessment and evaluation should not focus solely on outcome measures that are directed toward behaviors identified as success markers. Rather, they should be viewed as dynamic processes, integral to and subject to curriculum development and implementation. As such, assessment and evaluation can be described as educative processes having three distinct characteristics.

Continuous Process

Assessment and evaluation are continuous processes. One primary focus that describes assessment and evaluation processes in early childhood education is that they should be procedures that describe the progress of children over time. One cannot define what progress is, or describe it if evaluation is limited to assessing children only at the end of their experiences. By conceptualizing assessment and evaluation as continuous processes, the conceptualization of how children learn is implicitly affected as well. There is no inherent beginning, middle, or end to children's learning. While it may be important to identify the sequence that children are learning, what is also significant to recognize, and subsequently measure, is that children are progressing through the sequence, not necessarily that they are all at the same point in the sequence at some given moment. Education evaluation and assessment should be viewed as a description of where children are at any given moment within some learning sequence continuum. It is important to recognize, as well, that just as time continues on, so too does learning and the assessment of learning.

Comprehensive Process

Assessment and evaluation are comprehensive processes. Recall the story of the five blind men who experienced an elephant for the first time. After they had a chance to touch the elephant for a moment, each described to the rest of the group what he thought the elephant must look like. The first blind man who only touched the elephant's leg, thought that the elephant must look like a tree. After all, its skin was as rough as the bark of a tree and body as thick as a tree's trunk. After feeling the elephant's trunk, the second blind man was convinced that an elephant must look like a snake. It has no apparent skeletal structure and could move in wave-like motions. The third blind man, touching the elephant's ears, conveyed to the rest that he thought the elephant must look like a large fan. The fourth man said the elephant must look like a long rope, after feeling the tail. The last blind man, feeling the large body of the elephant, described the elephant to the other four men as a large round boulder.

What does this story tell us about the assessment of children and program evaluation? While none of the men were totally wrong, none of them were totally right in their descriptions of the elephant. Each of them was partially correct because each only partially experienced the elephant. While assessing young children and evaluating early education programs are much more complex processes than describing an elephant, there are some similarities. In addition to the many aspects of learning and development that can be assessed, there are many contexts within which they can be assessed. It is important to understand that evaluation should utilize multiple sources of information, assess multiple aspects of the individual, and take place in multiple contexts.

The above issue relates to a critical characteristic of assessment and evaluation in early education settings—the multidimensional aspect of learning and development, as well as the multidimensional aspect of the environments in which they occur. According to James Comer (1980), "People aren't educated in pieces, and kids don't learn in pieces. . . . That's why it's essential to address the entire social system of school because of the way many variables interact and . . . all affect school performance" (quoted in Schorr & Schorr, 1988, p. 235).

Integrative Process

Evaluation and assessment are integrated into the instructional process. It may be prudent to reiterate a number of earlier expressed statements to summarize the role of evaluation in the instructional process. The instructional goals expressly stated in the curriculum should guide the process of evaluation. The nature of what is assessed and how assessment procedures are defined should be directly linked to what experiences children have within the curriculum. As will be discussed in chapter 8 on "alternative assessment," assessment and evaluation procedures can be subsumed within the instructional process itself.

There are two ways that the outcomes of assessment and evaluation are directly linked to instruction. First, evaluation and assessment can be used as tools for modifying curriculum to meet individual children's needs. As was discussed, all children benefit in different ways from different instructional strategies. Through evaluation we can better understand which children benefit from which instructional strategies. Second, evaluation can be used as a tool to measure overall curriculum effectiveness. Just as curriculum experiences are beneficial to different children in different ways, there may be some curriculum experiences that are effective for no children. Evaluation can also be a useful instrument in making general curriculum adjustments, as well.

*

In this chapter, the role of assessment and evaluation in early childhood was discussed from various perspectives. It was described as having various but related purposes and characterized as a process, integrated into curriculum development, implementation, and modification. In addition, the importance of considering the unique characteristics of the child and curriculum as they relate to assessment and evaluation were explained. In chapter 3, a detailed discussion of the relationship between early child development and assessment will be described.

Evaluation from a Developmental Perspective

In the 1920s and 1930s it was commonly assumed that infants were blind or at least minimally sighted at birth. One of the leading reasons for this belief was that behavioral scientists at the time were not very good at "asking questions" of infants and often applied assessment techniques that were appropriate for older children. When the infant "failed" these tests, the assumption was either that the behavior did not exist or the infant was incapable of performing the behavior. Not until infant development and behavioral competencies were better understood were more developmentally appropriate and therefore more accurate assessment techniques created.

While this represents a blatant example of a mismatch between the child's development and the assessment technique, more subtle instances exist in early childhood as well.

One of the primary ways that preschool children are evaluated is through the use of teacher directed questions. In a study of teacher-child discourse Blank and Allen (1976) found that up to 50% of the language that teachers use in the classroom are teacher posed questions. Conventional wisdom was that if children did not answer the question appropriately or at all, they did not have the "right" answer. A number of studies have found that there is, in fact, a developmental sequence that determines the types of questions children can comprehend (Cairns & Hsu, 1978; Gullo, 1981; Tyack & Ingram, 1977). The following order has been established: "yes-no" questions; "who" questions; "what" questions; "where" questions; "when" questions; "why" questions; and "how" questions.

This order represents increasing levels of abstractions required to comprehend what type of information is being requested.

For example, the concepts related to "who," "what," and "where" are concrete referents related to persons, places, and things. These are concepts that children acquire early. On the other hand, concepts related to "when," "why," and "how" are abstract concepts related to time, cause-effect relationships, and manner, respectively. These are concepts that children acquire later, some-times not until 6, 7, or 8 years old. Yet teachers assume, many times, that "all questions are created equal" and do not selectively choose the types of questions they ask when assessing young children.

It was also found in a subsequent study (Gullo, 1982), that the order of questions listed above also represented increased levels of linguistic complexity required to respond appropriately to the ques-tion. To respond appropriately to the earlier developing questions (Yes-No, Who, What, Where), a single word response is acceptable and appropriate (e.g., yes or no, a person, a thing, a place). To answer When, Why, or How questions, children need to formulate more complex linguistic utterances to appropriately respond. The implication is that younger children, even if they know the infor-mation that is being requested of them, may not have the complex linguistic structures needed to answer the questions being asked.

The two examples described above, related to infant assessment and preschool question comprehension, illustrate the importance of child development and its relationship to individual assessment. They illustrate just how development can and appropriately should influence the process of assessment. Conversely, they also demon-strate the erroneous conclusions that may be drawn from assessment results if the child's development is *not* considered.

In an assessment policy statement, the National Association for the Education of Young Children (NAEYC) (1988a) states, in essence, that early childhood practices should reflect and take into account the child's level of development. Likewise, it should be rec-ognized that the developmental characteristics of children affect assessment and evaluation procedures and outcomes (Cryan, 1986; Gullo, 1988, 1990; Meisels, 1987). The manner in which this prin-ciple impacts curriculum development and implementation is well documented (see, for example, Bredekamp, 1987; Gullo, 1992). It is imperative, however, that the assessment and evaluation procedures and processes be considered an integral part of the curriculum in the early childhood classroom.

DEVELOPMENTAL CONSIDERATIONS

Under both formal and informal assessment and evaluation conditions, it should be recognized that the developmental characteristics of individual children, or the characteristics of a group of children within a particular developmental period, affect how they will respond in and to various assessment and evaluation situations. In this chapter, four such developmental considerations will be discussed.

Developmental Constraints on Responses

First, it should be recognized that there may be developmental constraints influencing children's responses in certain assessment situations. When children in early childhood settings are assessed in order to determine whether or not they have acquired specific information during a particular instructional experience, it should not be assumed that an inappropriate response or no response at all indicates that they do not have the sought after information. One of the things that should be considered if this occurs is whether or not the method used to assess the child is consistent with the child's individual and general age-related developmental capabilities to respond.

If, for example, the assessment method requires that the child use extremely controlled fine motor movements (e.g., fill in a small bubble on a sheet with many pictures and other bubbles), the inability to exhibit movements such as these may actually impede the child's ability to demonstrate that he or she has acquired the knowledge being assessed. Similarly, the language used by an adult or another individual to assess a child's performance may not be consistent with the child's own level of language development, or the adult's language may not reflect content that is familiar because the child comes from a very different background. In this situation, the question is not meaningfully stated for the child, who will not respond in the anticipated manner even if the information or skill being assessed is known or has been acquired.

Another developmental trait of children during the early childhood years is that they demonstrate impulsive behaviors more than do children who are at more advanced levels of development. Impulsivity means that children will often respond with the first thing that comes to their mind without reflecting on or considering alternative responses. This "thinking without reflection" leads younger children to respond in assessment situations in ways that are not consistent with adult expectations. "Multiple-choice type" assessments using pictures provide a good illustration. One typical item on such an assessment might require a child to look at a picture and then circle one in a following row of pictures that goes best with the first. Typically, on items such as these, the test developers might place a "decoy" picture first. This is a picture that, if there wasn't a subsequent "better" choice, would be the "best" response. The young child might be disadvantaged with this type of test structure because he or she might select the first picture that meets the requirements of the task and never consider the choices that follow.

In summary, the child's level of social, language, cognitive, and motor development often affects how he or she will interpret and respond, during both formal and informal assessment situations. Therefore, we must take this into account when we interpret their responses.

Differences in Motivation

A second important developmental consideration is that the motivation to do well in evaluative situations differs depending on children's level of developmental accomplishments as well as their experiential backgrounds. We know from experience with children and youths, as well as from research, that motivation to do well accounts, in part, for one's performance in that situation. Young children often don't understand the importance or significance of their performance in these formal or informal assessment situations. Many times, the reinforcement or incentive to perform is simply to complete the task, so that they can go on to a more comfortable or enjoyable circumstance. There is little that can be done, in general, to convince a 5-, 6-, or 7-year-old that their performance during certain evaluations may have long-range consequences on their academic future. What we should be aware of, however, is that children's "lack of motivation" to perform according to external standards and expectations may influence their behavior in these situations. It should be understood that lack of motivation is not meant in the pejorative sense. Rather it is due to children's lack of understanding or appreciation for the significance of the task.

There are some groups of children, however, who have more experience with "assessment-like" situations, and therefore, may be more motivated at earlier ages than others to perform well. Children who come from middle socioeconomic status (SES) backgrounds are more likely to have been engaged in these types of situations than children who come from homes of economic poverty. Because they are more likely to have had these types of experiences before, in their homes, as well as in other types of settings, they may be more comfortable answering questions, or being-assessed in other ways. Familiarity alone could account for these children being more at ease and therefore more motivated to do well in an assessment situation.

Exaggerated Perception of Performance

A third developmental consideration is that there are differences in how children perceive themselves as compared with how others perceive them relative to their performance on various tasks. An important element in the evaluation of children's performance is the degree to which children incorporate feedback into the internalized assessment of their own competence. Research suggests that younger children's perception of their own competence is inconsistent with teachers' ratings of their competence (Gullo & Ambrose, 1987; Stipek, 1981). Teachers anticipate that the critical feedback given to children is used by them to gauge future behaviors. But this is a misconception. It is not clear that young children, below the age of 8, perceive the feedback as criticism, or that they use teacher feedback focused on academic performance to determine or modify their future behaviors. Research has found that young children uniformly have an exaggerated perception of their own abilities (Gullo & Ambrose, 1987; Stipek, 1981). Nicholls (1978) found that not until sixth grade do children's perceptions of their abilities closely reflect their actual performance. Children's ratings of their own performance do not begin to correlate with teacher ratings of children's performance until about 8 or 9 years of age (Nicholls, 1978, 1979).

A developmental explanation for this phenomenon exists. From a Piagetian framework, Stipek (1981) concludes that preoperational children may confuse the desire to be competent with reality. Because most children do not get feedback regarding their competence that is either all good or all bad, they are left with mixed messages regarding their actual performance status. Preoperational children are then left to judge their own competency level based upon inconsistent and ambiguous feedback from the teacher. Piaget (1925) describes children of this age as having an exaggerated feeling of self-efficacy. This may be due to the egocentric nature of the preoperational child. Children at this age tend to concentrate on and pay attention to that which is salient to them. When they receive evaluative feedback from the environment, both positive and negative, they may focus on only the positive, thus getting a false sense of competence. Apple and King (1978) suggest that teachers of young children tend to focus on school behavior and social adjustment when giving feedback to the children rather than provide reinforcement on the basis of the quality of the children's academic performance. The child may use this feedback to evaluate his or her competence in cognitive and academic performance as well. Thus, young children may get little direct and meaningful feedback regarding their academic performance.

Differences in Generalizing Knowledge to New Concepts

A final developmental consideration is that there are differences in how children generalize their performance or knowledge from context to context. It is not appropriate to assume that because children's performance in academic settings indicates that they possess knowledge or skills within one particular context, that they will be able to generalize this knowledge or skill and demonstrate it in all contexts. This reflects a developmental phenomenon known as vertical decalage (Phillips, 1975). For example, if children are only provided with experiences using mathematical concepts and operations in contexts where they manipulate objects but never have opportunities for using representational symbols, these children may not be able to demonstrate what they know when assessed representationally, with paper and pencil tasks. Therefore, it is imperative that children be given opportunities to experience knowledge and skills in many contexts, both concretely and representationally.

While it is true that children in the preoperational stage of development acquire new knowledge and skills when given concrete experiences with real objects, it is important that they be allowed to practice and/or generalize these newly acquired skills and knowledge in many different contexts. The implication here is twofold. First, we must not assume that because a child can demonstrate a competence in a particular context, that he or she has completely incorporated and internalized the understanding of this knowledge or skill enough to demonstrate it in all possible contexts. Conversely, we must not assume that because a child does not demonstrate a called upon competency during an assessment situation, that the child would not be able to demonstrate the knowledge, skill, or process if requested to do so in an appropriate context.

ASSESSMENT AND EVALUATION CONSIDERATIONS

In his book, *School Power,* James Comer (1980) states, "The most basic problem with education today is the assumption that if the kid doesn't learn, it's the kid's fault. The school doesn't take the responsibility" (cited in Schorr & Schorr, 1988, p. 237). While Comer was referring to broader issues related to educational systems, an important lesson can be gleaned from his statement with regard to assessment in early childhood education.

The first error in making the assumption that children don't learn is not knowing how to determine *if* they have learned. If they "fail the test," the conclusion is that they obviously haven't learned anything. Some children are more vulnerable to this faulty reasoning than others.

In this section, a number of developmental considerations have been presented and discussed. The aim is for this information to shed new light on assessment, so that when children "fail the test," educators will think, "did we ask the right questions?"

The developmental and curricular principles and issues discussed in this chapter and in chapters 1 and 2 are significant in assisting early childhood educators to make appropriate decisions regarding assessment and evaluation. There are many types of assessment and evaluation procedures available for use in early education settings. The type of procedure chosen by the early childhood educator should take into account a number of factors.

First, what is it that is going to be assessed? Some things are more reliably assessed using one procedure over another. For example, if a teacher is trying to determine the number of procedures or steps children take to solve a particular problem, this might be considered an assessment of a process, rather than a skill. It may be more appropriate to use a more informal assessment technique in this situation. If, on the other hand, a teacher is trying to determine what information children have already acquired in order to plan curriculum activities, a more formal technique may be appropriate.

Second, what are the children's developmental characteristics that will be assessed? How do these developmental characteristics relate to what is being assessed? As was discussed previously, the developmental immaturity of some children, or the lack of linguistic or fine motor competence of others may preclude the use of some assessment techniques. The developmental characteristics of children must be taken into account when selecting assessment procedures and interpreting assessment results.

Third, what is the intended use of the assessment information? If the intended use is to describe certain behaviors or academic skills or processes, then the score from a more formal assessment procedure would probably not be appropriate. If, however, the intended use is for the determination of an individual's ranking on a particular skill or informational task, then a more "formal" assessment score may be the more appropriate avenue to take.

Fourth, who will be implementing the assessment procedure? Some assessment procedures require no specific training. Others require very specific training and skills. It must be determined if the person executing the assessment or evaluation procedure possesses the necessary skills to adequately accomplish the task.

∗

In Parts II and III, respectively, formal and informal assessment and evaluation procedures related to early childhood education will be discussed. Processes and instrumentation, along with associated issues will be presented.

Part II

The Role of Formal Assessment and Evaluation in Early Childhood Education

CHAPTER 4

Formal Assessment and Evaluation Instruments and Procedures

In this chapter formal assessment and evaluation procedures will be discussed as they relate to early childhood education. Types of formal assessment as well as characteristics of formal assessment and evaluation instruments and procedures will be detailed.

Formal assessment and evaluation instruments generally refer to those that are standardized. In early childhood education, three types of standardized assessments are used: developmental screening tests, readiness tests, and diagnostic tests. The standard referencing of these tests falls into two categories—norm-referenced tests and criterion-referenced tests. Similarities, differences, and what to consider when choosing between the two types of tests will be discussed. Important characteristics of standardized tests will also be described. These include reliability, validity, and practicality, which are important characteristics to examine when selecting an assessment instrument and/or procedure.

GENERAL CHARACTERISTICS OF STANDARDIZED TESTS

Prior to discussing specific types of standardized tests, it is perhaps important to consider standardized test instruments and procedures in a more general manner. A standardized instrument is one that generally has the following format and procedural characteristics:

1. It has a specifically stated purpose. According to the American Psychological Association (1974), "the test manual should state explicitly the purpose and applications for which the test is recommended;" and "the test manual should describe clearly the psychological, educational, and other reasoning underlying the test and the nature of the characteristic it is intended to measure" (pp. 14, 15).
2. There should be established procedures for administering and scoring the test. Any problems with administration or exceptions to the administration procedures should be clearly described.
3. There should be a description of how to interpret the test results. The test manual should give clear directions on how to meaningfully compare an individual child's score with another's.
4. There should be a description of the sample population on which the experimental version of the test was developed. This is an important consideration. If the comparative scores on the test were based on a "white, middle-class, urban, upper Midwest" sample, the comparison of an individual child's scores might be meaningless if the child comes from a largely "African-American, lower socioeconomic, rural, Southern" region. One should examine the test manual to determine if the sample used to develop the test is representative of the population at large, or appropriate for the specific population being tested.
5. Any limitations of the test should be stated in the test manual. Again, if the test was developed using a narrowly defined sample, it would be valid for use with children matching those characteristics but might have limitations when used with other types of children.

TYPES OF FORMAL ASSESSMENTS

In early childhood education there are many reasons to use formal assessments. The overall goal should be to inform curriculum and instruction. That is, by using the information derived from the tests, we can learn more about children and can use this knowledge for modifying the curriculum to meet individual children's needs. The three types of formal assessments and reasons for their use that will be discussed in this section are developmental screening tests, readiness tests, and diagnostic tests.

Developmental Screening Tests

According to Meisels (1989b), developmental screening in early childhood education "is a brief assessment procedure designed to identify children who, because of risk of possible learning problem or handicapping condition, should proceed to a more intensive level of diagnostic assessment" (p. 1).

In a related article, Meisels (1987) states that there are primarily two purposes for developmental screening. The first is to identify those children who may be in need of special educational services. The second is to identify those children who might benefit from a specialized educational plan within the "regular" classroom. In this manner, a developmental screening test is used to measure children's potential for learning.

In their position statement on standardized testing of young children, NAEYC (1988a) states that developmental screening tests are inaccurately labeled as such and are in actuality "developmental tests." These two views are not dichotomous, they both wholly agree on two aspects. First, that these tests measure certain skills and behaviors that children have already acquired. Therefore, such things as motor development, language development, and conceptual development might all be assessed on a developmental screening test. Second, they both agree that the results of developmental screening tests are often misused. This practice can lead to inappropriate placement of the child within the early childhood setting or, even worse, can prevent the placement of children in programs.

Generally, developmental screening tests are norm-referenced assessment instruments that allow one to compare an individual child's score with those of other children of similar chronological age. Many of the available developmental screening tests vary somewhat in their focus. Meisels (1989b) states, however, that most of the test items on the screening instruments can be grouped into three areas.

In the first area, items are related to visual-motor and adaptive skills. These involve such things as control of fine motor movements, eye-hand coordination, the ability to recall sequences using visual stimuli, copying forms from two-dimensional representations of the form, and reproducing forms from a three-dimensional model.

The second area involves skills related to language/communication and thinking. The tasks here include language comprehension and expression, reasoning, counting, and recalling sequences from auditory stimuli.

Finally, the third area includes gross motor skills and body awareness. This involves such things as balance, coordination of large muscle movements, and body position awareness.

The greatest misuse of developmental screening tests stems from using instruments that are neither valid nor reliable (Meisels, 1987). Both reliability and validity will be discussed later in this chapter. Suffice it to say for now, that a reliable test is one that is consistent in what it measures. A valid test measures what it purports to measure. Many of the developmental screening tests that are used are teacher constructed instruments. These tests usually do not undergo psychometric research to establish their validity and reliability. Therefore, it is not always easy to accurately ascertain what the test measures.

While developmental screening tests that are both valid and reliable can measure children's learning potential, research has indicated that the ability to predict future school performance declines over a 2-year period (Meisels, Wiske, & Tivnan, 1984). Meisels (1989b) summarizes the limitations of developmental screening tests the following way. Data from developmental screening should only be viewed as preliminary information regarding children's development. Diagnostic or assessment decisions should not be made using screening instruments alone. There are a number of misuses that should be avoided when using the results of screening tests. These include using screening information to make decisions regarding school entrance, using the score on a developmental screening tests as an IQ score, or labeling children based upon their score on a screening test. Meisels also cautions that screening instruments should not be used with populations to which they are not sensitive (e.g., culturally, linguistically, or socioeconomically different children). In addition, developmental screening should not be done outside of the educational context, which includes assessment, evaluation, and intervention.

In appendix A of this book, examples of developmental screening tests are described. These descriptions include what is covered in the test as well as who is qualified to administer the test.

Readiness Tests

Readiness tests are used in early childhood education to assess the degree to which children are prepared for an academic or preacademic program (NAEYC, 1988a). They are similar in form and content to achievement tests in that they both measure children's mastery over specific curriculum content. However, readiness tests do not assess this to the extent that an achievement test would in either depth or breadth. Achievement tests are used primarily to determine children's mastery over curriculum content after a period of instruction, while readiness tests assess what content children have mastered in order to determine how "ready" they are to go on to the next phase of instruction. Most readiness tests are criterion-referenced and have items that focus on general knowledge and skill achievement and performance (Meisels, 1987).

According to Meisels (1987), many people confuse readiness tests with developmental screening tests. They are similar in that both are brief and are used as a sorting device to some extent. However, Meisels points out that the purpose of the two is very different. As stated earlier, the purpose of a developmental screening test is to sort out those children who may be in need of further diagnostic testing in order to determine if they require special education service. The purpose of a readiness test is to determine the specific skills and knowledge children have mastered. The results of readiness tests are used for both placement and curriculum planning. As such, readiness tests are product oriented—measuring what skills and knowledge the child already possesses—while developmental screening tests are process oriented—measuring the child's ability to acquire new knowledge and skills (Meisels, 1987).

Because readiness tests do not directly measure children's potential for future learning, they do not adequately predict future academic achievement. (Wiske, Meisels, & Tivnan, 1981). Simply stated, a readiness test cannot validly be used to predict future academic success in children. Instead they describe children's current level of academic knowledge and skills.

A number of readiness and achievement tests commonly used in early childhood education are described in appendix A. As will be noted, many are group tests and are administered by the classroom teacher or trained paraprofessional. The intended use of each of the specific tests along with a description of what is assessed by the instruments is included. A comprehensive discussion of the psychological constructs underlying readiness will be presented in chapter 6.

Diagnostic Tests

A diagnostic test is used to identify the existence of a disability or specific area of academic weakness in a child. Test results are used to suggest possible causes for the disability or academic weakness as well as suggest potential remediation strategies.

Unlike many developmental screening or readiness tests, diagnostic tests are usually administered by highly trained individuals such as school and clinical psychologists, speech pathologists, social workers, guidance counselors, and teachers. A child who is undergoing diagnostic assessment may be seen frequently by a group of professionals known as a multidisciplinary assessment team.

As stated earlier, developmental screening should not be used for diagnostic purposes. While many of the same types of behaviors are assessed by both instruments, screening devices are very limited and brief, while diagnostic instruments have a much more comprehensive scope.

Some diagnostic instruments may be specialized and used when a specific learning problem is indicated. For example, if a child has language that is unintelligible, what might be warranted is a diagnostic articulation test. If the child has intelligible speech, but has poor conceptual or other general language difficulties, a different type of language assessment might be called for. If, on the other hand, the child demonstrates general cognitive delays, an IQ test or other measure of cognitive abilities may be warranted.

In appendix A, a number of diagnostic instruments are listed and described. As will be seen, the scope of the tests varies as do the ages of the children that they are intended for. Some of the instruments are very specialized by developmental domain while some are general. Some are specialized by specific age range while others are appropriate for early childhood through adulthood.

*

In the next section of this chapter, specific characteristics of formal assessment and evaluation instruments and procedures will be discussed. The understanding of these concepts will make the user and interpreter of assessment and evaluation outcomes better prepared to make choices and decisions regarding children and curriculum.

STANDARDIZED REFERENCES FOR TESTS

Designers of standardized tests must consider certain characteristics when developing the measures. One of the primary characteristics considered is the standard reference to which children will be compared. In this section, two such standard references will be discussed.

Norm-Referenced Tests

Norm-referenced tests are used when one is interested in comparing a child's performance with those of a representative group of children. (Boehm, 1992; Wortham, 1990). The children with whom the comparison is made may be of a similar age or grade level.

The primary use of norm-referenced tests is to make educational decisions for children related to selection and classification (Boehm, 1992). Most intelligence tests and achievement tests are examples of norm-referenced, standardized tests.

Cryan (1984) states that there are three principal reasons for using norm-referenced tests. First, they should be used to assess the individual on information that is not sequential and where no specific level of competency is essential for making educational determinations. Second, they should be used when there is a need to choose an individual from among a group because a norm-referenced test will give teachers information regarding a child's relative performance. Finally, a norm-referenced test is used when it becomes imperative to examine individual differences. Because the scores are standardized according to some criterion, they provide an equal basis from which to compare.

The scores on a norm-referenced test may be reported in a number of ways. Below are listed some of the more common methods of reporting scores on standardized, norm-referenced tests.

Standard Scores. Standard scores permit the comparison of a child's performance on one test to his or her performance on another test. The standard score is derived statistically using the child's actual performance score and comparing it to the average score and theoretical range of scores to be expected for the population.

Percentile Scores. Percentile scores indicate an individual child's ranking in the distribution of scores indicated by the comparison group. It indicates what percentage of the comparison group scored either above or below the target child's score. For example, if a child received a percentile score of 72, it would indicate that this particular child scored better than 72% of the children that he or she was being compared to and lower than 28%. Conversely, if a child's percentile ranking was 26, it would indicate that 74% of the children in the comparison group received higher scores.

Age-Equivalent Scores. An age-equivalent score indicates the average chronological age of children achieving a particular score on a test. If, for example, a child who has a chronological age of 5 years, 8 months receives a raw score on a test that translated into an age-equivalent score of 6 years, 2 months, it would mean that this score was 6 months above what would be expected for a child of his or her age.

Grade-Equivalent Scores. Grade-equivalent scores are closely related to age-equivalent scores except that the comparison is by grade level rather than by chronological age. Often the grade-equivalent score is reported in years and months. A grade-equivalent score of 2–6 means that the score attained would be one that would be expected from the average child in the sixth month of second grade. Comparisons among children can be made using grade-equivalent scores as is the case with age-equivalent scores.

Criterion-Referenced Tests

Unlike norm-referenced tests, criterion-referenced tests are not concerned with children's performance relative to a comparison group. Rather a criterion-referenced test measures the degree to which a child has attained a certain level of accomplishment according to a specified performance standard. Often, criterion-referenced tests are used to determine the effects of instruction, and performance standards can either be in the form of behavioral or instructional objectives.

Boehm (1992) discusses two major advantages to using criterion-referenced tests. First, this form of assessment is concerned with children's mastery over instructional skills, knowledge, or processes. It does not concern itself with the comparison of children. Second, the results of criterion-referenced tests more easily translate into instructional goals. Contrasted to a norm-referenced test, where the performance score does not indicate how the child achieved the score, the criterion-referenced test is specifically related to the child's performance on an instructional sequence. Therefore, individualizing instruction is facilitated.

Gronlund (1973) lists several standards against which criterion-referenced measures should be compared. These standards are detailed in Boehm (1992), and include criteria regarding the tasks measured, the sequential presentation of tasks, and the standards by which children are judged.

First, the tasks measured should be clearly defined. In doing so, the behavioral criteria that are to be used as evidence of having achieved a level of competence should be operationalized so that they can be reliably observed and measured. If it proves difficult to decide whether or not a child is exhibiting a particular behavior, then perhaps this criterion has not been met.

Second, a detailed task analysis description of the expected sequence of behaviors should be provided. This will be achieved using some type of categorical structure of behaviors. Behaviors may be grouped sequentially under such headings as fine motor skills, problem-solving skills, communication skills, or social skills. It should also be noted whether or not an adequate sampling of behaviors under each of the skill areas has been used.

Third, the standards by which children are rated should be clearly stated. As such, the criterion levels that indicate "success" should be specifically outlined. In this manner, the results of the scored assessment should describe the child's behaviors clearly.

According to Cryan (1986), there are a number of conditions to consider when making the decision to use criterion-referenced tests. Criterion-referenced tests should be used when

1. Educators are interested in locating specific areas of difficulty that children are having related to curricular performance. This might include locating strengths as well as weaknesses.
2. Educators are trying to determine proficiency or competency levels in children. This would be important to ascertain when determining their next level of instruction.
3. The skills or processes that make up the subject being taught are sequenced. Sequencing may represent increasing levels of complexity (such as the steps necessary to solve problems requiring different mathematical operations) or simple ordering or quantifiable sequencing (such as the necessity to learn the names of many different shapes and/or colors before more complex processes can be attained).

PSYCHOMETRIC CHARACTERISTICS OF STANDARDIZED MEASURES

In order to determine whether or not a particular standardized measure will be useful for a particular educational situation, there are a number of psychometric properties of the instrument that should be considered. In this section, a number of these properties, along with their implications, will be discussed.

Test Validity

Test validity is the degree an instrument assesses what it purports to assess. It is important to know about an assessment instrument's validity in order to determine how useful the information taken from the test will be in making inferences. There are a number of different types of validity that may be reported in the test manual.

Content Validity. Content validity refers to the extent to which the test's content is related to the intended purpose of the test. For example, in a reading readiness achievement test used in early childhood education, the content would be the curriculum content, instructional strategies, and curriculum and instruction goals. By providing information on content validity, test developers are defining the extent to which items in the test assess the objectives outlined in the test, thus fulfilling the purpose of the test (Wortham, 1990).

Knowledgeable assessment consumers should likewise determine the extent to which the expressed objectives and the purpose of the test matches their curriculum content, instructional strategies, and overall goals.

Criterion-Related Validity. Criterion-related validity provides evidence that the resulting scores on a particular assessment instrument are related to one or more outcome criteria. Two types of criterion-related validity are usually reported.

The first type is called concurrent validity. Concurrent validity refers to the degree the score on a test is related to the score on a different but similar test. For example, children's scores on one achievement test may be compared with their scores on a different achievement test. If the children's scores on the two tests are highly correlated, then they may be used as evidence of concurrent validity.

The second type of criterion-related validity is called predictive validity. The concern of predictive validity is with stability of the test score over time. It was reported earlier in this book that some developmental screening instruments do not have good predictive validity. That is, they may present a satisfactory measure of children's current development but they do not accurately predict their future status. If a test has good predictive validity, it can be used as an indicator of future scores when related constructs are assessed.

Test Reliability

Reliability is a measure of test consistency. That is, it is an indication of how dependable and repeatable the score of a given test is. The higher the reliability coefficient, the greater likelihood that differences in an individual's scores over repeated test administrations is due to test taker performance, rather than to test error of measurement. Three types of reliability can be reported.

Test-Retest Reliability. In test-retest reliability, a single form of a test is administered to a norming or experimental group for the purpose of establishing reliability. After a short interval of time the test is readministered to the same group and the scores from the first administration are compared (using correlational analysis) with the second set of scores. The correlation coefficient will be an indication of how closely the scores from both administrations are related. If the correlation is high and positive, it is an indication that the test was consistent in measuring its objectives.

Split-Half Reliability. In split-half reliability, the norming or experimental group is administered the test for which reliability is to be established. The scores on one half of the test are compared (using correlational analysis) with the scores on the second half of the test. If the correlation coefficient is high and positive, this is an indication that the test is internally consistent in measuring the same objectives.

Alternate-Form Reliability. There are situations when it is appropriate to have two different forms of a test, with both forms designed to measure the same characteristics. The *Peabody Picture Vocabulary Test* and the *Metropolitan Readiness Test* are two examples of tests that have alternate forms. It may be important to have alternate forms of a test if it becomes necessary to administer a given test to the same group of children during a very short period of time. If you administer the exact same form of the test, confounding variables, such as familiarity with the content or a practice effect, may influence the scores. In alternate-form reliability the two alternate forms of the test are administered to a single group of children. The second form of the test is administered after a short interval of time. The scores on the first form of the test are then compared with the scores on the second form of the test in much the same manner as in the other two types of reliability described above. A test with high positive alternate-form reliability is an indication that either form can be used interchangeably.

Assessment Practicality

Although validity and reliability are important psychometric qualities of assessment instruments that should be considered when selecting a test, the assessment tool's practicality must also be considered. This is the degree to which the teacher or others can utilize the information derived from the assessment instrument to make decisions about children and/or curriculum and instruction. There are two questions to consider when deciding on the practicality of the assessment.

First, how well do the objectives of the test match the objectives of the curriculum and instructional strategies used in the early education setting? Just as it seems foolish to use a hearing test to determine visual acuity, so it is foolish to use an assessment instrument that is not related to the curriculum that the children are participating in. If the curriculum and assessment are not closely related, analysis of the test outcome will do little to help teachers use the results of the analyses for curriculum development and/or modification.

Second, how well does the test (content and procedures) match the developmental characteristics of the children for whom it was intended? The issue here is how valid and reliable a test is in its relation to the developmental stage of the child. That is, it is generally true that because young children are not good test takers, the younger the child is, the less likely it is that the test will be reliable and valid. This factor must be considered when choosing tests and interpreting test results. Chapter 7 in this book details the developmental characteristics of children that must be considered when making decisions about testing.

NAEYC (1988a) also relates the lack of reliability and validity in tests designed for young children to the rapid rate at which these children develop. This necessitates repeated assessment administrations both often and in different contexts if accurate and up-to-date information is to be available for decision making. Cryan (1986) and Shepard and Smith (1986) point out that when this issue is not considered, the result is inappropriate placement of children and detrimental labeling.

✻

As users of tests and test results, teachers and others working in early education settings must become informed consumers of early childhood assessment instruments and findings. When they are not, potential dangers exist. Knowing which type of standardized measure to use and understanding its psychometric properties represents only part of what one should consider. Other inherent dangers in the use of standardized tests must also be examined. Chapter 5 discusses those dangers along with things to consider in making informed decisions regarding early assessment.

Making Informed Decisions About Formal Assessment and Evaluation

Individual assessment of children in early education settings is not, nor should it be, disappearing. Unfortunately, neither is the inappropriate use of assessment and evaluation information, not so long as testing and its perceived significance are as prevalent as they are in our early education system. According to Gnezda & Bolig (1988), testing at the prekindergarten level is mandated by as many as 16 states. Additionally, prekindergarten testing is required by district mandate in as many as 37 states.

With the practice of testing children in early education becoming so widespread, so too are the deleterious effects that accompany testing's misuse. A number of the dangers associated with the misuse of testing will be discussed in the first part of this chapter. This will be followed by suggestions for how teachers and others working in early education settings can become informed users of tests and their findings.

DELETERIOUS EFFECTS ASSOCIATED WITH THE PRACTICE OF TESTING

Effects on Curriculum and Instruction

Over-reliance on the test or test results could have an adverse affect on the curriculum. Teachers may inadvertently or deliberately teach to the test in order to increase the scores of the children in their class. This has the effect of narrowing the curriculum so that the learning of information tested by the test becomes the primary curriculum goal and objective. Meisels (1989a) labeled this practice "high-stakes testing." High-stakes testing adversely affects the curriculum and subsequently the children.

While one effect of "high stakes testing" is to narrow the curriculum within an individual classroom, another harmful effect of testing associated with this curriculum practice is when assessment and/or evaluation entirely determines the program. Madaus (1988) refers to this as "measurement-driven instruction." Some school systems use test results for teacher and program accountability. In order to increase the likelihood of higher test scores, teachers will then often base their decisions on what to teach and how to teach it on what information and processes will be assessed by the end-of-the-year test. The effect of this is to narrow the curriculum to those topics that are covered by the test or are most subject to being measured by a test.

Meisels (1989a) cautions that this practice often results in a curriculum and instruction style that is rigid and lacks creativity and imagination. It also has the effect of moving the curriculum away from being child-centered to being content-centered—that is, the content that is covered on the test. Madaus (1988) continues that if instruction is measurement driven, the teacher is relinquishing responsibility for curriculum development to those who design the tests; in essence giving test publishers control over the school curriculum. This practice may even determine the sequence that curriculum content is taught in.

I recall a kindergarten teacher, "Ms. Smith," with whom I taught during my first year in the public schools. At the end of each school year, a standardized test was administered to all kindergarten children for the purpose of planning the following year's instruction. Once it was known that each classroom's scores would be made available for examination by other teachers, parents, and other interested parties, the seriousness with which teachers entered into this annual ritual dramatically changed.

One year "Ms. Smith" was determined that her class would be at or near the top of the score distribution. She perused previous years' test results to determine what sorts of information was most troublesome to her students. She then focused her activities on the concepts and skills that she determined would have the biggest pay-off for increasing test scores. "Ms. Smith" even moved her unit on Native Americans from autumn (Thanksgiving) to spring (closer to the actual time of testing) and planned a field trip to the local museum of natural history solely for the purpose of "teaching" her class what a moccasin was. No child in any of her previous classes had known what a moccasin was. She was determined that her children would get that item correct on the test this year. Talk about narrowing the curriculum!

While this story illustrates an extreme case, even minor infractions of this nature are antithetical to sound practice in early education that is grounded in developmental theory. What must be strived for is using tests to serve educational practice rather than determining it.

Effects on Children

Inappropriate use of assessment information can have detrimental effects on children. One of the most costly errors that can occur is when testing leads to inappropriate labeling. As has been discussed earlier and will be discussed further in subsequent chapters, young children are not reliable test takers. Again, a developmental rule applies here—the younger the children the less reliable they are as test takers. One test that has recently come under scrutiny, The Gesell School Readiness Test demonstrates that test results can lead to inappropriate labeling in young children (Meisels, 1987, 1989a).

The Gesell School Readiness Test is administered to children prior to kindergarten entry. The score that the children attain determines whether they are labeled "ready" or "not ready" to learn in kindergarten. It has been argued that the test may indicate what information the children have already learned, but not the extent to which, or the rate at which new information can be learned. To this extent, tests may be able to paint a picture of what information has already been acquired by children, but test scores tell us little about children's rates of learning, modalities through which they learn, or the nature of their reasoning processes. Yet assumptions are made about children's cognitive processes on the basis of their score on a particular test. Many call this readiness.

As early as 1966, Bruner questioned the whole notion of readiness. On one hand, we tend to assess whether or not readiness exists in children, as though it were an inherent biological trait. On the other hand, we recognize readiness in practice as a modifiable environmental trait, something that you can teach and nurture. Time alone is not sufficient to create the existence of readiness in children. In chapter 6, an in-depth discussion of this concept and its relationship to testing will be presented.

Aside from resulting in inappropriate labeling of children, testing may also cause us to view the nature of children's progress in fragmented and compartmentalized ways, rather than in cohesive and integrative ways. While current trends in early childhood education are calling for curriculum practices that view progress as continuous and integrated, tests force us to artificially determine beginnings and ends of instructional sequences. This practice is simply used to facilitate the assessment of children's progress.

Finally, we should be aware that many tests measure a restrictive range of learning and development. What we come to understand about children as the result of this kind of testing will be as narrow as the range of behaviors that are being assessed. There are at least two ways that tests reflect a narrow picture of children.

First, a test may be restrictive in the extent to which a particular skill or developmental domain is actually measured. When one thinks about the complexity of skills and processes involved in the development of language or cognition in children, it would be difficult to conceptualize an assessment instrument that could account for all of those complexities. While a particular test may be both reliable and valid, it is incumbent upon the user of the test to determine what it is that is actually being measured and not to interpret beyond that level.

Take, for example, a test of cognitive development, the results of which classify a child as being in one particular stage of cognitive development, say either preoperational or concrete operational. How does the test assesses this? What skills or processes does the test measure to make this determination? What skills does the test not measure? It is known that children may exhibit characteristics of being in more than one stage of cognitive development. This is known as decalage. If the children are not given the opportunity to demonstrate higher order skills and processes, we come away with a restrictive view of their developmental accomplishments. While a test like this may prove useful in certain situations, caution should be taken not to overextend the findings to contexts that are not applicable.

A second way a test may be restrictive in portraying children is when the social context that is reflected in the test content or procedures is discrepant from the one that the child is developing and learning in. Again, while this information may prove useful in a limited context, the question that again must be asked is, what information do children have or what skills do they posses that are not being addressed in a particular test?

In summary, then, we should be aware that tests, either standardized or teacher made, are restrictive in the portrait that they paint. Therefore it is important not only to assess children's learning and development according to what tests tell us about them, but also to assess them in light of what the test is unable to inform us about them.

Effects on Professional Trends

There is a fashion adage that says if you wait long enough, everything eventually comes back into style. In educational practice, this is sometimes referred to as a pendulum effect, where certain educational practices come and go, according to whim or societal conditions.

Recently, Meisels (1992) identified yet another type of trend associated with early childhood practice and usually the direct result of testing. He refers to this as an "iatrogenic effect." According to Meisels, iatrogenics is a medical term that describes a potentially harmful or unwanted side effect accompanying the intended effect of medical treatment.

Certain harmful educational practices in early childhood education have come to be associated with the practice of early grade testing. Despite intended useful practices that can be associated with appropriate uses of test results, too often negative effects also result.

Raising the Mean Age in Class. As was discussed above, as many as 37 states have school districts that require testing in prekindergarten. Many of these districts use these test results as guidelines for parents to make the decision whether to send their child to school that year or wait an additional year. The result of this is that some children enter kindergarten at age 5, while others enter at age 6, even though they were of legal entry age at 5. The curricular trend that accompanies this practice is that in order to maintain the expectations at a level that accommodates the mean age in the class, requirements to perform in an "average" manner are raised to accommodate the older average age in the class. This makes it more difficult for the young 5s in the kindergarten to function in an average way because they are expected to act older than their actual age.

School systems have responded to this dilemma by systematically raising the legal entry age requirements. Shepard and Smith (1986) report that during the last decade, school districts gradually moved the entrance age for kindergarten back. The effect of this is that the average age of children entering kindergarten has gotten older and older. Some specific examples may prove useful.

Wolf and Kessler (1986) did a survey of the entrance ages required by states and how they changed during an 8 year period. In 1978 they found that 15 states required that a child be 5-years-old by September in order to be unconditionally enrolled in kindergarten. The other 35 states permitted children to enroll in kindergarten who would not be 5 until later than September. By 1986, the number of states that required children to be 5 by September rose to 26.

In a more dramatic case, the state of Indiana's automatic entrance age for kindergarten is now "5 by June 1" (Meisels, 1992). This practice went into effect in 1992 as the result of a 1 month rollback each year for 3 years.

While the practice of raising the average age in class seems like an adjustment of sorts, the effect is that it changes the role and function of early education. In addition, it affects the expectations of what should occur prior to school entrance as well. While some children may be positively affected by such practices, many children, particularly those who reside in homes of economic poverty, may find themselves falling farther and farther behind. If this practice continues, the result may be separate educational systems, a condition some would say already exists.

Retention and Transitional Programs. When schools rely heavily on tests for placement of children, retention and transition classes are two ways in which they deal with children they judge "unready" for a more "formal" curriculum. While transition programs (2 years of kindergarten or 2 years of first grade) are thought to lessen the stigma associated with retention, they can be considered retention, nonetheless. According to Shepard and Smith (1988) regardless of whether it takes 2 years to get to first grade or 3 years to get to second grade, all 2-year programs can be categorized as retention. Shepard and Smith list a number of retention euphemisms: prekindergarten, developmental kindergarten, buy-a-year, begindergarten, transitional first grade, readiness room, pre-first grade, and academic redshirting.

While there is an intuitive conception that 2-year programs are beneficial for those children not considered ready for a traditional, more structured first-grade curriculum, research does not substantiate this contention. A number of studies that compared children who are in transition programs, with children who were eligible for transition programs but did not attend, showed no differences in achievement performance levels (Gredler, 1984; Jones, 1985). In a later study, Shepard and Smith (1987), examined groups of children who were closely matched on age, sex, and readiness scores, and found that children who participated in transition programs received a mere one month advantage on a number of variables when compared with children who went to schools whose systems did not participate in transition programs. These variables included reading levels, math performance, teachers' ratings of academic performance, self-concept, and attention.

While many studies seem to demonstrate that there are no realized benefits for children who participate in 2-year programs, some studies reveal that there could be detrimental effects. These negative effects fall into categories related to poor self-concept—negative attitudes towards school, feelings of failure, being bored, and being teased by peers (Bell, 1972; Shepard & Smith, 1985, 1987).

General Misuse of Testing Results

General misuse of testing results can create deleterious effects in any of the above three categories. There are a number of ways in which test results can be misused.

First, there may be an overuse of standardized tests. The concern over the overuse of standardized tests in early education is widespread (Wortham, 1990). Using standardized test results for teacher accountability, determining student participation in federally funded programs, comparing the quality of teaching among school districts, or as the basis upon which funding for schools is determined are all ways that have been cited as misuses of test results.

A second misuse, somewhat related to the first, is using standardized tests for a purpose not intended by the test developers. In one study, for example, Durkin (1987) found that teachers and administrators were using the Stanford Early Achievement Test (Madden, Gardner, & Collins, 1984) to determine which children should be promoted and which should go into a transitional class. This in spite of the fact that the Stanford Early Achievement Test was designed to measure the progress of students.

Many times a test manual will give equivalent scores. The Peabody Picture Vocabulary Test–Revised (Dunn & Dunn, 1981), an assessment instrument designed to measure children's receptive vocabulary ability, gives IQ equivalent scores in the manual. Many mistakenly assume that this means that the test can interchangeably be used with an IQ test. It is important to remember to use the test results only as intended and described in the test manual.

A third misuse of standardized test results occurs when the test has been given to a population for which it was not intended. It is difficult to find a test that could be considered culture-free, one that is not biased to either give an advantage or disadvantage to children of a particular cultural, racial, economic, ethnic, or linguistic group. The results of tests must therefore be interpreted with this in mind.

Finally, although standardized tests have established procedures, one cannot be assured that the tests are administered uniformly. In this way the results may be misused because they were inappropriately obtained. This can especially occur if they are group administered tests given by a number of different classroom teachers. Testing early childhood aged children proves even a greater challenge for group testing because difficulties related to attention, individual differences, fatigue, and distraction are exacerbated in group administered early childhood standardized tests.

The preceding discussion of the problems that can arise in the administration of standardized tests and the misuse of their results is not exhaustive. The issues presented here are meant to serve as a structural guide for thinking about the problems and misuses of standardized tests. Further misuses of test information are discussed elsewhere in this book.

INHERENT DANGERS IN THE PRACTICE OF TESTING

Along with the practice of testing in early childhood education comes inherent dangers that can result in the negative effects discussed above. Two of the most critical of these inherent dangers are as follows.

First, test administration as well as scores themselves are subject to both human and environmental error factors. As has been discussed in an earlier chapter, young children are not good test takers. There are many developmental and environmental conditions that may affect test performance and subsequent score. For example, young children are language bound. That is, they rely on the language of the test and administration directions to guide them through the procedures and lead them to making appropriate responses. Unfortunately, while the "language of the test" may be perfectly clear to those who develop the tests, often young children misinterpret what is expected of them and this often leads to inappropriate responses.

Interpretation of test results are also subject to human error. Teachers seldom delve into an item analysis, and thus they rely on the total scores achieved by the children as indications of their performance levels.

Test scores are also subject to environmental factors. The configuration of items on a page, the number of items on a page, or the manner in which items are depicted are all factors that may affect children's performance. Again, the younger the children are, the more this is true. Often standardized test formats alternate between presenting the sequence of items in a row and in a column. This may have disastrous effects on children who are "used" to one format or the other. If there are too many items on a page, it is not difficult for young children to lose their places or get out of sequence with no awareness that they have done this.

Awareness that both human and environmental factors affect children's performances on tests may prove helpful in overcoming this danger, but even if the danger can't always be overcome, at least the importance of test outcome can be put into perspective.

A second danger associated with the practice of testing in early childhood education is that formal assessment measures seldom inform us about children's rates of learning, modes of learning, or their problem solving abilities. As has been discussed in chapter 3 of this book, young children's performances in early education settings can be both stylized as well as reflect individual characteristics of the child. These characteristics include varying rates of maturation, individual learning styles, and different approaches to solving problems. Unfortunately, tests are used within single formats and meant to be appropriate for all children in a particular group. While the test may be able to provide information regarding what factual information children have (within the parameters of the test questions), tests are not individual enough to meet the developmental needs of each particular child.

Tests given at the conclusion of an instructional unit assume that all children require the same amount of time to process the information and acquire the knowledge or skills that unit addresses. This is a faulty assumption. Tests do not permit a divergence of problem solving paths. As such, important information about children may be lost or assumed unimportant.

While early education programs may "preach" and even practice (within curriculum design and instruction) developmentally appropriate programs, that by definition include individualization and modification based upon developmental needs, these programs often use rigid assessment practices and assume homogeneity of rates and styles of learning. This further exacerbates a problem that exists in early education today—that of viewing assessment and evaluation as separate from curriculum. As this book has suggested throughout, if early education professionals are to fully integrate curriculum and assessment, then they must fully "practice what they preach."

BECOMING INFORMED USERS OF ASSESSMENT TECHNIQUES AND INFORMATION

There are a number of things that early childhood professionals should consider when using tests and/or interpreting assessment information. Many of these suggestions have their foundations in what has been discussed previously in this book or will be discussed in subsequent chapters. Therefore, some of the suggestions from the following list are meant to serve as a review, while others are meant to serve as a preview of forthcoming discussions. In addition, by re-categorizing the information in this way, it casts a new light on its significance. It should be noted that these suggestions pertain to the more "formal" and structured assessment procedures such as standardized and teacher-made tests.

1. Select only tests that have demonstrated validity. It is important to determine that the assessment instrument tests what it purports to measure. As such, tests should only be used for their intended purposes and in conjunction with other types of assessment information. This is crucial for curriculum planning as well as for determining child progress.

2. Select only tests that have demonstrated reliability. This is important because it insures that the information garnered from the assessment results are not spurious. Again, for making decisions about children and/or curriculum, be sure that the findings are consistent.

3. Consider readiness test results as only one source of information to assist with appropriate curriculum planning. While the readiness test may indicate where the child's academic performance level is at a given moment, NAEYC (1988b) states that children should not have to conform to rigid homogeneous group expectations. Rather, groupings for specific activities should be flexible and change frequently. Therefore, observation of children's performance within group activities serve as important sources of readiness information.

4. Never use test scores as the sole basis to determine placement. NAEYC (1988b) suggests that children should be allowed to enter school based upon their legal right to enter and upon their chronological age, not based upon what knowledge they have acquired. Further, NAEYC contends that promotion and placement in special programs should be based upon multiple sources of information.

5. Gather assessment information about children on a regular basis. As has been stated, children learn at different rates and

do not conform to the rigid schedules for learning sometimes imposed upon them by curriculum and teachers. Therefore, it is important to regularly determine, not simply at the end of an experience, information about children's academic and developmental accomplishments.

As has been discussed in this as well as in previous chapters, it is incumbent upon the consumer to become an informed user of tests. In early childhood, the consumer must not only be aware of the test's traits, but also of the traits of the children for whom the test is intended. In addition, the user must also understand fully how the test results will be used. A primary use of the test results in early childhood is to determine children's readiness. In chapter 6, the relationship between testing and readiness will be examined.

CHAPTER 6

Testing and School Readiness

According to the National Association for the Education of Young Children (Bredekamp, 1987), ongoing assessment and evaluation in early childhood education occurs primarily to determine children's curricular needs. Others advocate that certain types of assessment and evaluation may be used for other purposes (e.g. Uphoff & Gilmore, 1986), particularly for children just entering kindergarten. They propose that children be evaluated to determine whether or not they are "ready" for school. A central assumption of this position is that children should be homogenously grouped in school, according to developmental level rather than chronological age. Thus, if a child is of legal entry age for kindergarten, but tests at a younger developmental age, the child should presumably be given the "gift of time," or another year, to become ready for the curriculum. Readiness is central to this issue, yet there are many interpretations of the underlying constructs defining readiness.

WHAT IS READINESS?

Readiness is a term often associated with early childhood education. Its use, however, is not standardized. The concept is often used to describe how prepared children are to start "formal schooling," start "formal reading instruction," start "formal math instruction," or move on to the next grade level. In this regard, one interpretation of the readiness concept utilizes assessment to determine whether or not children are ready for a particular experience. If it is determined that children are not ready, it may preclude them from participating in some experiences.

In another interpretation of readiness children are assessed to determine what experiences they are ready to encounter. This interpretation is consistent with principles of developmentally appropriate practice and would not prohibit children from participating in any educational experiences, but would suggest that educational experiences be modified to meet children's developmental needs.

This latter interpretation of the readiness concept is also more consistent with what we know about children's development because readiness is determined by the child's development and it is known that in the early years children do not develop at a consistent rate.

Three general rates of development patterns can be observed in typical children. There are the fast start children. These children mature very early and rapidly. By the time they are 5 and entering kindergarten, they may be reading (or very ready to read), have their fine motor behaviors under control, be socially mature, and display language and problem solving capabilities that are advanced for their age. These children may start to plateau by the time they reach 6 or 7.

The next pattern of development results in the even start children. Their development, if plotted on a graph, would result in a gradual upwardly sloping line. They develop precisely according to age norms, most of their behaviors are age appropriate, and they continue to develop in this gradual manner throughout the early childhood years. Academically, these children are on grade level most of the time.

A third pattern of maturation that can be observed in children's early development results in what could be called slow start children. These children develop slowly in the early years. By the time they are 5 and entering kindergarten, they may demonstrate clumsy fine motor development, social immaturity, and seemingly delayed language and cognitive abilities. These children, given supportive and facilitative physical and social environments, often experience increases in their rates of development by the age of 6 or 7.

While the descriptions of these three rate patterns of typically developing children are both generalized and theoretical, they have some very important implications regarding how assessment and evaluation might affect children. While in prekindergarten, kindergarten, and first grade, teachers could expect differences in academic performance among the three groups of children described above. But by the time these children reach third grade the expectation would be that many of these differences would have disappeared—that is, if one holds with the current tenets concerning child development. However, in practice, this usually will not occur—most times differences have not disappeared. It is possible that teacher assessments of pupils in lower grades have caused the teacher to treat the "slow starters" differently from the "fast" and inadvertently reinforced developmental differences and solidified student status.

Another problem educators must be aware of is that the practice of testing to determine developmental level for purposes of school readiness and entrance, constitutes, in my opinion, both a class and a gender bias. Children from economic poverty and boys, in general, will be over-identified by developmental readiness instruments as those in need of the gift of time. Both socioeconomic status (SES) and gender have been shown to correlate with scores on tests such as these (Shepard & Smith, 1988).

According to Piaget (Inhelder, Sinclair, & Bovet, 1974), children's construction of knowledge and problem solving abilities, two processes assessed in tests used for the purposes described above, are the manifestation of the interaction among the developmental factors of maturation, physical and social experience, and equilibration. Although maturation is biologically determined, the remaining two factors are not. Therefore, a child's score on a developmental readiness test is only partially the result of the maturational process. Still, those who advocate the gift of time maintain that maturation alone—or time—is sufficient to bolster a child's developmental level and knowledge sufficiently to prepare him or her for the kindergarten experience.

Much of the variance in readiness test scores among groups of children is due to the types of self-selected or societally-selected experiences each child has had, not from differences in level of maturity. Thus, the belief of gift-of-time advocates that they are segregating out children who lack the appropriate maturational level necessary for success in early schooling is erroneous. What they are segregating out are those who have not had the appropriate physical and social experiences that most kindergarten curricula require as measures of success—and in all likelihood, the kindergarten class may be the only place where these children can receive these experiences.

Assessment instruments such as those used to determine gift of time children, examine development as though it can be photographed and scrutinized at that frozen moment in time. In essence, the assessment ignores the child's past physical and social experiences that have influenced the responses. In addition, it cannot determine what type of experiences the child may require in the future, or how the child will benefit from those experiences.

EFFECTS ON CHILDREN OF SCHOOLING DECISIONS BASED UPON THE "GIFT OF TIME"

Schooling decisions based upon the gift-of-time testing position take various forms. One is to prohibit children's entrance into kindergarten for an additional year. Another is to place children into what has come to be called a "developmental kindergarten," which is the 1st year of a 2-year kindergarten track. These children will thus spend 2 years in kindergarten before being promoted to first grade. Still another is the transitional first grade. In this format, children identified as "not ready" will spend 2 years in first grade before being passed into second. Both of these forms of early childhood "retention" were discussed more completely in the previous chapter.

The schooling practice most often associated with the gift of time, is the delaying of children's entrance into kindergarten for an additional year. As with kindergarten entrance testing, this practice represents a classist and sexist bias, and has the potential for impeding the development of those children who are most in need of the experiences they will miss. This is particularly true for children from economic poverty, and others who come from environments that do not afford them the types of experiences they require for even modest success in today's schools.

It will be recalled, cognitive development is not only the product of maturation, but also the result of the interplay of maturation with physical and social experiences. Children from economic poverty who are kept out of school for an additional year will probably not undergo the kinds of experiences they need to prepare them for school. On the other hand, middle SES children denied entrance to kindergarten are much more likely to encounter the kinds of enriching experiences they need before entering school. Thus, by keeping both these children out of school, the developmental gap between children from environments of relative advantage and disadvantage is likely to widen even more.

According to Kozol (1990), the practice of tracking children has similar effects. Children who are tracked into a 2-year kindergarten or a transitional first grade are likely to be denied the experiences they require to advance. Such tracking becomes, therefore, a type of segregation, in which the poor in the lower tracks "cannot impede the progress of the more privileged children" (p. 52).

Devotees of schooling practices based upon the gift of time believe that children are given the "gift" to allow them to mature and prepare them for a more successful early school experience. In reality these practices often become a "theft of time," especially for those children who most need the physical and social experiences that a developmentally appropriate kindergarten curriculum can provide.

TEACHING, CURRICULUM, AND THE "GIFT OF TIME"

The gift-of-time phenomenon has the potential to adversely affect, not only children, but the nature of the kindergarten and subsequent primary curriculum. By testing all children and excluding those whom an instrument deems not ready for kindergarten, we are engaging in the first step of "high-stakes testing" (Meisels, 1989a). This concept was introduced earlier. According to Meisels, we are engaging in high-stakes testing if we are using tests to exclude children from kindergarten who are of otherwise legal entry age. Moreover, by only including those children in kindergarten who meet a given criterion level, we may promote an escalation of the kindergarten curriculum itself (Shepard & Smith, 1988). It then follows that there will be an escalation of subsequent first, second, and third grade curricula as well. In this manner, the gift-of-time practices have resulted in the early childhood curriculum becoming

test driven and more academically skill oriented, another characteristic of high-stakes testing.

As has been indicated in chapter 5, one outcome of this situation has been a steady increase in the average age of kindergarten
children. This occurs for two reasons. First, parents have been more
likely to keep their children out of school for an additional year, so
that their children are the "smartest" in the class. This primarily
tends to be a middle class phenomenon, to occur more with boys
than with girls, and to occur most with summer born children. Second, because of the escalation of the curriculum, more and more
school districts are raising the minimum entry age for kindergarten.
This constitutes another example of a "theft of time," particularly
for those children who are in most need of it. While middle SES
children may fill the year with preschool experiences or enriching
experiences at home, many children from economic poverty will
simply wait and lose more precious time. Thus, the vicious cycle of
widening the academic gap between children of means and those
of economic poverty continues.

The gift-of-time concept also has the potential effect of homog-
enizing both the kindergarten classroom and curriculum. If only
those children who are the most developmentally able are permitted
into the kindergarten classroom, the result will be fewer individual
differences among children and a curriculum tailored to go along
with it. But teaching only the most developmentally ready children
makes teaching easier, and thus this concept is getting support from
some kindergarten teachers. This is especially true when teachers
are pressured, and evaluations of their teaching abilities are based on
their pupils' standardized test performances.

THE RIGHT PROBLEMS BUT THE WRONG SOLUTIONS

"Kindergarten requires children to sit quietly, to take turns, to work
with workbooks and ditto sheets. But a lot of children at that age
need more freedom to move around to play." According to Louise
Bates Ames, one of the early proponents of the gift of time, this
describes the kindergarten of today (Uphoff & Gilmore, 1986, p.
31). Uphoff and Gilmore also lament that the typical contempo-
rary kindergarten causes undue stress, lowers self-esteem, and cre-

ates other emotional and psychological problems in young children. Their solution is that "anyone under the age of 5 years, 6 months has no business in a formal classroom" (p. 6, emphasis added).

Most professionals in the field of early childhood education would not argue with these positions, especially if a "formal classroom" means that every child must be doing the same thing at the same time; every child must be instructed primarily in teacher directed, large group settings using worksheets; and every child's timing of progression through the curriculum is determined by his or her test score. A "formal classroom" of this type has no business in kindergarten!

According to the gift-of-time advocates, the solution for reducing kindergarten imposed stress is to fix the children—that is, to give them more time so that they are better able to handle the stress. They specifically contend that children below the developmental age of 5 years, 6 months, as determined by testing, are simply not ready for kindergarten. In reality, it's not a matter of readiness on the part of the child; it's a matter of the kindergarten curriculum not being developmentally appropriate for children of legal entry age for school.

Gift-of-time advocates also suggest that the younger children in kindergarten classrooms are being set up for failure. But, according to Shepard and Smith (1988), their solution of raising the entry age merely exacerbates the curriculum problem. The effect of raising the average age of kindergarten children will almost certainly create a situation where even more inappropriate curriculum and instruction practices will be "pushed down" into the curriculum from the higher grades. Again, the youngest will suffer. Raising the entrance age is not the solution, for there will always be a youngest in the class.

One cannot argue with the basic premises that (1) bad starts in school often lead to difficulty in school later; and (2) being required to perform at levels beyond your developmental capabilities leads to stress, frustration, and low self esteem. To this end the gift-of-time advocates make all the right points, identify all the right problems, but consistently come up with all the wrong solutions. To reiterate, the problem is not with the children, it's with the kindergarten curriculum.

The solutions to these problems are best put forth in NAEYC's (1988b) position on what schools can do to ensure that all children get off to a sound start. The following is suggested:

1. That all children enter school on the basis of their chronological age and legal right to enter school rather than on the
   basis of what they already know.
2. That teacher-child ratios should be low enough to allow
   teachers to individualize instruction and not expect that all
   children do the same thing at the same time.
3. That if children are grouped, the groupings should be flexible and change frequently so that the children don't have to
   conform to rigid expectations.
4. That children should be allowed to progress at their own
   pace through the curriculum.
5. That the curriculum and teaching methods be appropriate
   for the age and development of the children in the class.

One way early childhood professionals have responded to the testing dilemmas discussed in this and the previous two chapters, has
been to augment, and sometimes replace formal assessment and
evaluation instruments and procedures with informal assessment
and evaluation procedures. In Part III, the role of informal assessment and evaluation in early childhood education will be the focus
of discussion. Included will be issues related to alternative or
authentic assessment and the roles that they play in early education.

Part III

The Role of Informal
Assessment and
Evaluation in
Early Childhood Education

CHAPTER 7

Informal Assessment and Evaluation Procedures

In this chapter, informal assessment and evaluation procedures will be discussed. These will include direct observation, the use of interviews, questionnaires, and checklists, as well as collecting samples of children's actual classroom work. In the two chapters following, systematic methods for using informal assessment in early childhood settings will be presented. In chapter 8, the discussion will focus on organizational methods, such as portfolios, and process methods, such as observing and recording children's work in problem solving and project tasks. Chapter 9 will focus on ways for using various classroom contexts as assessment and evaluation opportunities.

DIRECT OBSERVATION

Direct observation, the most basic of all informal assessment techniques, often requires active participation on the teacher's part during daily classroom routines when children are engaged in curricular activities. While teachers often don't trust their powers of observation to inform them about children's strengths and needs, research has demonstrated that when teachers use observation techniques as a basis for their ratings of children's academic strengths, those ratings correlate highly with objective measures of children's academic performance (Gullo & Ambrose, 1987).

According to Wortham (1990), observation procedures afford teachers the opportunity to assess certain behaviors in young children that more formal assessment procedures do not. In early child-hood education, teachers are often more concerned with children's learning processes or the processes they use to acquire new information, rather than with what specific information has been learned. More formal test formats do not allow one to determine the processes that occur in young children's minds. Therefore, observations of children solving problems or sorting objects may give greater insights into these processes than do test scores alone.

Furthermore, young children have often not mastered the language or behaviors required to perform adequately in a structured test situation. Therefore, observing them in a more natural environment may give a better indication of their competence.

Finally, observation procedures offer a better channel to evaluate children's development, and early childhood educators are particularly interested in assuring that there is a match between the child's development and educational goals and materials. Therefore, a reliable and valid procedure for assessing development becomes a vital aspect of assessment and evaluation in early education.

Forms of Observation

Observation can take many forms. The form selected should be suited to the situation and setting, as well as to the teacher's skills and needs. Each of the different types of observation appropriate for use in early education will be briefly described.

Anecdotal Records. Anecdotal records are brief, narrative descriptions of specific events. According to Boehm and Weinberg (1987), anecdotal records should be used for understanding behavior when there are no other means to evaluate it directly. These behaviors might include such things as attitude towards learning, emotional development, peer relationships, or effects of health on children's adaptation to school settings.

For example, a group of public school, prekindergarten, and kindergarten teachers with whom I work use anecdotal records as a standard procedure in their student assessments. A 5 x 8" note card is kept for each child in the class. The cards for the entire class are held together using a ring-type fastener. Each time the teachers observe something that they have predetermined as important in describing individual progress or in achieving a curricular objective, it is noted on the card. Teachers might note such things as symmetry in block building, patterns established with beads or blocks, colors and designs used in art projects, social interactions between children, or language used.

The teachers use a team approach and the anecdotal record cards are discussed with aides and specialists who service the rooms. Suggestions for curricular activities, modifications, and further things to look for are typical topics of discussion. The cards are divided into six categories of behaviors, including language and literacy, logic and mathematics, movement, initiative, social relations, and creative representation.

Cartwright and Cartwright (1984) and Goodwin and Driscoll (1980) have suggested a number of characteristics anecdotal records could have as well as procedures for developing them.

1. An anecdotal record should be the result of direct observation of behavior, and the recording should occur as promptly as possible following the event.
2. An anecdotal record should only include the description of a single event.
3. An anecdotal record should include contextual and supportive information to assist in interpretation at a later time.
4. The interpretation of the behaviors observed should be done separately from the recording of behaviors and events described in the anecdotal record.

Running Record. A running record is closely related to an anecdotal record, however, it is more detailed and represents a sequence of behaviors rather than the description of a single incident. Boehm and Weinberg (1987) note that running records may be useful in describing small changes in development or in behavior. Because the observation is continuous over a specified time period, this procedure can become time consuming. Cryan (1986) suggests that often the use of audio or video recordings of behaviors aid in the process.

Time Sampling. Time sampling is used when there is interest in determining the frequency of a certain behavior. In a time sampling procedure, children are observed for a predetermined period during which the specified behavior is recorded each time it occurs. This observational technique may be especially useful for observing children who exhibit problematic behaviors. For example, it might be important to determine how many times the child exhibits aggression or withdrawal during a specific time period, to better plan for their educational needs.

Event Sampling. Event sampling is used instead of time sampling when the context is the main point of interest. Rather than observing for behaviors during a specified time period, behaviors are observed during a specified event. Continuing with the example described above, it may be important to know that there are certain contexts when a child exhibits more aggressive outbursts than others. This would provide the teacher with useful environmental information to help plan for that child. Wortham (1990) suggests that one use event sampling when interested in determining cause-effect relationships between context and behavior.

For example, the teachers I described above, who use anecdotal record cards, have determined that, for some children, particular settings or contexts might be useful in providing important information. If a child is having difficulty in exhibiting prosocial behaviors during recess, the teachers will make it a point to observe that child every day during recess in order to note the social interaction that occurs.

Analyzing the Observation Situation

According to Vasta (1979), before engaging in any observational technique, one must consider four questions. First, what will be observed? While this seems like a simple question, it can become rather complex. For example, when observing a single child it is often difficult to determine how much of the other children's behaviors must be observed and recorded to best understand the target child's behavior. It is also important to determine ahead of time what specific behaviors will indicate what the teacher is trying to observe. What is important here is to understand that observation is not synonymous with lack of structure. There need to be clear targets and goals for the observation to be useful.

Second, when will the observations be made? The importance of this question is obvious for event sampling, but there are also important implications for other types of observation. Central to this question are concerns about the length and timing of observation. The child must be observed for some period of time and it will be important to determine how long a period of time is adequate to be a representative sample of behavior. Also related is, with what frequency do observations have to be made in order to give an unbiased behavioral sample? If observations are made only in the morning or only in the afternoon, the timing and single opportunity may confound the conclusions based on these observations. Again, these issues must be addressed prior to observation, but perhaps can only be resolved during the process itself.

Third, which observational method will be used? In response to this question, the teacher-observers must first determine what kind of information they are seeking and then choose the method of observation that will best give them this information. In many instances a combination of observational methods may best suit the situation.

Finally, how will the accuracy of the observations be verified? While this may be a difficult question to answer, in some ways it is the most important. The observer must determine if what is being recorded as observed is an interpretation of behavior or an actual accounting of behavior. Often the teacher can verify what was observed by involving multiple observers or through multiple source means. That is, the observation of the behavior may simply lead to further questions or conclusions that are best assessed through formal assessment means.

Advantages and Disadvantages of Direct Observation

The use of direct observation of children's classroom behaviors for purposes of assessment has both advantages and disadvantages. One prominent advantage is that as an assessment procedure, observation does not interrupt the process of educating children. Instead, it is accomplished during classroom time while children are engaged in curricular activities. Another advantage is that it represents a means of assessing children while they are engaged in learning activities in a more natural setting. Learning is assessed during the learning process. A third advantage of observation is that it affords an opportunity to assess a child in a variety of contexts. Small group, large group, or individual work time present different challenges to children. Observing a child in each context may provide useful information as well as a greater breadth of information for making curricular decisions for that child. Observing a child in a problem solving situation using concrete materials as well as in a situation using representational materials provides insights into that child's level of logical thinking.

While observation provides vast flexibility, it has some potential disadvantages as well. Questions regarding the validity of observations are sure to arise. That is, how can one be certain that the behavior that is observed really represents what it is interpreted to represent? Therefore, validity is tied to issues surrounding interpretation of the observation. Teachers vary in their observational skill and training. These factors alone may affect the validity of the observation.

Another potential disadvantage is observer bias. If a teacher sets out to observe a certain type of behavior in a child because of preconceived notions about that child, instances of that behavior may be observed and recorded where it really doesn't exist.

Finally, even an accurate observation may be taken out of context if the context is not readily known or apparent.

To illustrate this very important point, I am reminded of the story of the 4-year-old preschooler who was observed during free choice time. The teacher noted that the child chose to paint at the easel, almost every day. There was nothing too unusual about this, as many preschool children are drawn to this art medium because of its novelty. What was unusual, the teacher noted in her observation of the child, was that the child only used the color black. The teacher decided to continue this event sampling procedure. For a week, the child painted only using the black paint. The teacher was convinced that this was a sure sign of an emotional problem or a terrible home situation. Now, if the teacher had left it at that, she might have continued to assume that the child was troubled. However, the teacher decided that she should talk to the child's parents and perhaps get to the root of the "problem." The parents were at a loss to explain the etiology and suggested that the teacher ask the child directly why he only used black paint. Taking the parents' suggestion, the teacher asked the child (in a gentle manner of course) why he only used black paint when he painted pictures at the easel. "Because it's the only color I can reach," the boy replied, "you put the other colors too high-up."

CHECKLISTS

Checklists are instruments used to record and examine sequenced series of behaviors or skills usually directly related to educational or developmental goals. Checklists can be used by teachers to determine what skills children have or what developmental characteristics they currently possess in order to better plan for the next step. According to Wortham (1990), checklists are best used when a great number of behaviors are to be observed.

Checklists can include a variety of descriptive characteristics (Cryan, 1986). These include such behavioral categories as descriptive statements of traits, specific developmental characteristics, social/emotional behaviors, interests, specific academic skills, specific knowledge, or specific concepts. As such, checklists can either describe behaviors of a general nature (e.g., problem solving skills, social skills, critical thinking skills, attitudinal characteristics) or of a specific nature (e.g., word attack skills, steps in performing a science experiment, skills required to perform a specific motor sequence, concepts required to perform mathematical operations).

Checklists prove particularly useful in preparing children's progress reports. If designed carefully, the progress reports could be a subset or an abbreviated version of the checklists. In appendix B, an example of how one school developed a progress report using an observational checklist is presented.

Checklists also are helpful in providing information to parents regarding their child's progress.

Checklists, if well designed and used appropriately, can be a guide to understanding children's development and for developing curriculum. There are advantages to using checklists for these purposes. One advantage is that they are easy to use and provide a method for assessing individual children. It is usually easy to determine if a behavior or skill exists in an individual child, and by using a checklist format, one need only to keep track using a check or an "x." A separate checklist could be kept for each child, thereby enhancing the process of individualizing the assessment process. Another advantage of using a checklist is that it provides a clear visual image of children's progress. By coding or dating the observations, it is easy to determine how children are progressing in the specific areas described on the checklists.

There are also disadvantages to using checklists. If the sequence of skills or concepts do not match the curriculum goals, then the information collected would be useless at best and somewhat damaging to the curriculum at worse. If one makes the assumption that those characteristics described on the checklist must be vital (or they wouldn't be on a checklist), then the curriculum might be inappropriately modified to reflect those characteristics. This difficulty occurs primarily when commercially available predetermined developmental or academic checklists are used. The other side of the coin is that teachers must have a thorough understanding of the sequence of behaviors or skills required to perform a task or produce a product when they construct checklists. This takes careful research on the part of the teacher or a committee responsible for the instrument construction.

Finally, Wortham (1990) cautions that checklists are not, in and of themselves, assessment instruments. Rather they are an organizing mechanism for describing curriculum or developmental sequences. What is important is how the teacher uses the information regarding what characteristics or traits are present or absent in a child to develop curriculum activities for that child.

RATING SCALES

Rather than documenting the existence or nonexistence of particular behaviors or traits in children, rating scales are used to describe the degree to which those behaviors or traits are believed to be present in the individual. Rating scales are often used to measure those traits not easily described using other assessment procedures. For example, on report cards children's conduct, motivation, effort, and ability to get along with others is often described using a type of rating scale. The child may be rated in each of the above areas using the following:

1—superior
2—above average
3—average
4—below average
5—unsatisfactory

The major difficulty, and therefore an inherent problem, is that the ratings can become very subjective. Also, there may be descriptive terms used in the rating scales that have ambiguous references, and this increases the incidence of subjectivity.

Both checklists and rating scales describe behaviors without addressing how they are influenced by possible causes or contexts. Therefore, checklists and rating scales are best used in conjunction with other observational forms to provide a more comprehensive assessment picture.

EXAMPLES OF CHILDREN'S ACTUAL WORK

Collecting samples of children's work is another example of informal assessment. One way of systematizing examples of children's work for purposes of assessment is organizing it into a portfolio. Creating portfolios as an organizational method is discussed in detail in chapter 8.

There are a number of advantages associated with using collections of children's work. According to Cryan (1986), children's work provides teachers with real and direct, rather than contrived evidence of their progress or evidence that is extrapolated from a means other than classroom material. Further, if the examples of work are collected and dated, they may be later used and interpreted by individuals other than the teacher who collected the work.

Decker and Decker (1980) also suggest that there are potential disadvantages to using actual examples of children's work. One potential disadvantage is storage. Given the number of children in a classroom multiplied by the number of representative examples of classroom work, the amount of material to be collected and stored, even for a short while, could become staggering. One potential way to solve this problem is to use advanced technology such as computer scanners. Then pictures, writing samples, and examples of problems can be scanned and kept on a disk until a printed copy is needed.

Another disadvantage is that it is difficult to know how many samples or which samples are representative of the child's competence. While informal assessment and evaluation procedures have demonstrated potential for use in early childhood education, mere collections of information may prove cumbersome and confusing. A difficulty in using informal assessment techniques lies in designing an organizational structure for increasing utility and meaningfulness. Alternative assessment techniques, as described in chapter 8, have been one way early childhood education professionals are trying to surmount some of these difficulties.

Alternative Forms of Assessment

One way the field of early childhood education addresses the issue of testing and assessment as well as the manner it fits into a curriculum that meets children's developmental needs is through alternative or authentic assessment procedures. Alternative or authentic assessment are terms to describe the types of assessment procedures and organizational structures that are being used in lieu of or in addition to "standardized" testing, or paper and pencil tests. These types of assessments are more descriptive in nature and take various forms. Rather than simply focus on the products of learning (e.g., the right answers), they also emphasize and strive to portray how children process information, construct new knowledge, and solve problems.

It should be noted that alternative or authentic assessment describes an organizational approach not a specific procedure. It does not "re-invent the wheel." Rather, it is an approach to assessment that helps individuals organize and make sense out of some of the various types of informal assessment procedures discussed in chapter 7. An alternative assessment approach provides the vehicle through which these various types of assessment procedures can be integrated and used in concert to describe children's progress. Several alternative assessment approaches are used in early childhood programs.

ALTERNATIVE ASSESSMENT APPROACHES

Portfolio Assessment

Some teachers use portfolios to chart and describe children's progress. Portfolios are a systematic and organized collection of children's work and can include writing samples, art work, running records of children's behavior, and samples of children's problem solving skills. These collections are used as evidence to monitor the growth of student's knowledge, their skills, and their attitudes (Vavrus, 1990).

There are three types of portfolios that have been used in early childhood classrooms (Mills, 1989; Vermont Department of Education, 1988, 1989). The first type, called the "works-in progress" portfolio, contains stories, artwork, and so forth, that the children are currently working on. The works-in-progress portfolio can become unmanageable within a short time because it potentially contains all of a child's work.

A second type of portfolio, called a "current year" portfolio, contains the selections of work that the child and teacher have mutually agreed upon as representing certain criteria. The work is analyzed by teachers to give them insights into children's levels of accomplishments and a better understanding of how to structure the curriculum experiences for the child's next step.

"Permanent portfolios" are the third type of work folder. The examples of work in these folders are highly selective in nature and will accompany children to their next class. Although the number of examples needs to be limited, they should give the next teacher a clear idea of the students' accomplishments and current levels of development and achievement.

According to Shanklin and Conrad (1991), there are three considerations when deciding what types of information to collect in children's portfolio folders:

1. What will the exemplars convey about the child's level of development and achievement?
2. How will the information gleaned from the exemplars help teachers make decisions regarding curriculum development and modification?

3. How will the process of collecting information to be contained in the portfolios help children better understand their own academic and developmental accomplishments?

While the actual types of information contained in portfolios may change as the curriculum focus changes, it is important that both product as well as process measures be constantly represented.

Finally, much has been written recently regarding quality standards for portfolios. Paulson, Paulson, and Meyer (1991) suggest a number of principles to consider in developing a portfolio system.

First, the process itself of selecting evidence to be contained in the portfolio should afford both students and teachers an opportunity to learn something about learning. Through the selection process, both are required to reflect about how the work or project demonstrates what has been learned, developed, or achieved.

Second, students are encouraged to be involved in the process of their own learning. In this manner, portfolios are done by students, rather than for students. Because students participate in selecting of work and project samples, they are taught to value their work and themselves.   .

Third, portfolios should reflect how children's work progresses over time. Rather than simply a listing or collection of work and tests (as the more traditional cumulative folder is), the portfolio should contain a wide array of evidence reflecting progress.

Fourth, in order to be effective and useful, portfolios should have a structure. A rationale, goals, standards, and a systematized procedure for selecting content should be considered part of that structure.

Fifth, the function of the portfolio may change from the beginning of the year to the end of the year. The work collected over that time span to measure progress and growth may differ from the work that is passed on to the next teacher as best evidence of the child's academic and development levels and growth.

Project Assessment

Another type of alternative assessment is to evaluate children's progress by assessing their knowledge and problem solving skills through observations of them in actual problem solving situations. "Project Spectrum" (Krechevsky, 1991) is an example of one such assessment procedure. The theoretical foundation that "Project Spectrum" is built upon Gardner's (1983) multiple intelligences theory. The strategy is to recognize that there is potential variation in all children and activities. The goal of evaluation in "Project Spectrum" is to identify children's domain—specific strengths in areas not necessarily addressed in traditional modes of assessment. According to Krechevsky (1991), "It is the responsibility of the educational system to discover and nurture proclivities. Rather than building around a test, the Spectrum approach is centered on a wide range of rich activities; assessment comes about as part-and-parcel of the child's involvement over time in these activities" (p.44).

A number of "Project Spectrum" features are consistent with characteristics of developmentally appropriate practice. These include:

1. The curriculum and assessment procedures become integrated. Early childhood practices that are developmentally appropriate view the relationship between curriculum and evaluation as transactional, that is, each simultaneously affects the other. By using activities embedded within the curriculum as the means to evaluate, and using the outcome of the evaluation as a method to modify the curriculum, this relationship becomes actualized.

2. The procedure embeds assessment into real-world activities that are meaningful to children. By putting the problem solving activity into a context for which children have a referent in reality, one is more likely to maintain the interest and motivation necessary to obtain valid and reliable results.

3. The procedures used are intelligence-fair—they do not rely solely or primarily on language and logical thinking. Also, children's styles of performance are identified. Just as children do not develop in compartmentalized ways, they also do not learn or demonstrate competence in this manner. And just as the curriculum must be sensitive to the multiple modes that children use to acquire and construct knowledge, evaluation must be similarly sensitive.

4. The procedures used identify and emphasize children's strengths. Rather than focus on what children don't know and can't do, they focus on what they can do and do know,

and this allows one to approach evaluation and subsequent curriculum development from a positive vantage point. The modus operandi is that all children can learn.

Curriculum Checklists

Another type of alternative assessment is the criterion-referenced curriculum checklist (e.g., Meisels & Steele, 1991). The purpose of such checklists is for teachers to document children's progress in acquiring various skills and accomplishments categorized according to certain curricular objectives. Teachers chart children's progress by observing their behaviors during classroom activities. The information is not used to compare one child to another, but rather, to describe a single child's growth. In chapter 7, a more detailed and general discussion of checklists is provided. An example of one type of developmental/skills curriculum checklist designed by a school is presented in appendix B.

ADVANTAGES OF ALTERNATIVE ASSESSMENT

Alternative assessment procedures have some distinct advantages over conventional assessment procedures. These advantages include the utility of information resulting from the evaluation process, the acknowledgment of individual children's developmental characteristics, and the link between evaluation, the learner, and the curriculum.

Alternative assessment procedures focus on developmental changes in children over time. These procedures enable teachers to identify and chart children's individual progress in the curriculum and the information gathered from these procedures promotes individualization of the curriculum.

Alternative assessment, properly used, measures children's progress against themselves and focuses on the individual rather than on groups of children. The key word is progress. The child's progress is measured against his or her own rate of acquisition of skills and knowledge. In more traditional testing-like evaluation procedures, children's performance is compared with others. For children in the early childhood years, this is not appropriate most of the time.

Alternative assessment procedures don't rely on the "one chance" opportunity for the child to demonstrate competence. By observing children frequently and in various early childhood settings, teachers have many opportunities to observe and record children's behaviors and gain insights into the settings, contexts, and types of activities that best facilitate learning for individual children.

Alternative assessment procedures provide a close match between the curricular goals and assessment outcomes. Thus, the resulting information is relevant for further curriculum development and modification. In fact, if used appropriately, alternative assessment procedures provide concrete, systematic means for curriculum modification, not only to meet individual student's needs, but also for recognizing "what works" and "what doesn't work." By using actual curricular activities as the evaluation means, a broader measure of curricular effectiveness can be assessed.

Another advantage of alternative assessment is that procedures don't interrupt the process of curriculum implementation. It is estimated that teachers spend approximately 14 hours per year preparing their students to take standardized achievement tests, 26 hours for reading tests and about 18 hours for teacher prepared assessment measures (Maness, 1992). This results in approximately 58 hours per year or 6% of instructional time being spent preparing students for and taking tests. Children in their early school years can be especially affected by these disruptions in routine. Because alternative assessment procedures are incorporated into the daily routine, the teaching-learning process is not interrupted. This provides more time and opportunity for curriculum implementation and horizontal expansion of the curriculum. In addition, it adds to the continuity of experience children at younger ages require.

These procedures encourage and facilitate reflective self-evaluation in young children. It will be recalled from a previous chapter that one of the developmental characteristics of young children is that they often do not evaluate themselves in the same manner others do, or at all. By allowing children to select "their own best work" to put into the portfolio, they have the opportunity to reflect on what they've done. When children talk about their choices with the teacher (why did they select the work they did?; what makes it their best work?; etc.), teachers gain the needed insights into how the children view their own competencies. It also allows children to share their perspective with others and be directly exposed to others' perspectives.

Finally, alternative assessment procedures provide concrete information to present to parents. In doing this, teachers can focus on what progress children have made during a given time period by presenting actual examples of children's work. It helps parents understand the developmental progression of where their child started, to where he or she has progressed, and where he or she will go next. It also gives parents a better understanding of what the curriculum is like in their child's classroom.

In summary, there are a number of differences between alternative assessment and conventional assessment procedures (Chittenden, 1991).

1. Alternative assessment procedures are ongoing, while conventional assessment procedures tend to be summative in nature.
2. Alternative assessment procedures use open ended formats, while conventional assessment procedures use closed, objective measurement procedures.
3. Alternative assessment procedures collect evidence from a variety of contexts, while conventional assessment procedures base their results on a single setting.
4. Alternative assessment procedures are mediated by teachers, while conventional assessment procedures are teacher proof.
5. Alternative assessment processes inform practice, while conventional assessment procedures verify practice.

STRATEGIES FOR DEVELOPING AND IMPLEMENTING AN ALTERNATIVE ASSESSMENT PROGRAM

It is important to plan carefully before drastically changing anything perceived as traditional educational practice. Educational evaluation is thought of in narrow terms, and any deviation from these may be greeted less than enthusiastically by those who have to implement the experiment. Not until recently has there been any attempt to describe the qualitative differences between evaluation in early childhood education and evaluation that occurs in later childhood education years. It is even more recently that an attempt has been made to create evaluation practices that parallel the qualitative differences described. Alternative or authentic assessment is one such attempt.

Although alternative assessment is not limited to a single assessment practice, it is possible to undertake common strategies to insure greater likelihood that the alternative program, however designed, will be successful. One way to measure success is to judge to what extent the program is used.

Create an Assessment Committee

An alternative assessment program should be "tailor-made" to fit the particular needs of the school and information should be collected from multiple sources in order to make it fit as closely as possible. Therefore it is necessary that individuals coming from diverse backgrounds, who directly and indirectly affect the children and their educational programming, be involved in developing the evaluation plan. Teachers representing each of the grade levels in the school would be essential members of the assessment committee, for they can discern what kinds of information could be collected at any time and what kinds of information would be unique to a particular grade level. They could also anticipate how the evaluation information and procedures fit the existing curriculum. Record keeping is an important part of evaluation, and teachers would be able to foresee how new procedures might be substituted for or added to existing ones.

School administrators are necessary committee members as well. They provide the support, both moral and financial, for school initiatives. Administrators who are convinced of the importance for change in early childhood evaluation will more readily provide such support. In addition, they can provide important feedback for what types of information are necessary for district reporting.

Specialists, in music, art, and physical education, and other fields, can provide important information regarding children's development. As such, they should be included on the committee.

Finally, parent participation is critical. Only parents can provide certain types of information. Unfortunately, parents are accustomed to and expect numerical or letter grades and scores to indicate to them how well their child is doing as compared with others at his or her grade or age level. Just as many teachers and administrators need to be convinced that describing children's progress is a viable and valid means of evaluation, so too, parents often need to be educated to this fact. Parents can offer suggestions regarding how this could be done. Their support is fundamental and extremely important.

Develop an Assessment Philosophy

It is imperative that each assessment program or plan has a philosophical basis to it. The philosophy sets the tone and direction. In developing the philosophy, the assessment committee should consider the following questions:

- Why do you assess in early childhood education settings?
- What will you do with the information collected during the evaluation process?
- How are the assessment procedures linked to the curriculum content and implementation strategies?
- What should the information collected during the assessment process tell about the child?
- What should the information collected during the assessment process tell about the curriculum?
- When should assessment take place?
- What is it that will be specifically assessed?
- What decisions about the child will be made as a result of the information gathered?
- What decisions about the curriculum will be made as a result of the information gathered?

By giving detailed responses to these questions, the assessment committee will develop, in essence, evaluation guidelines. These guidelines will, in turn, lead to decisions regarding evaluation materials and procedures.

Develop a "Standardized" Procedure for Implementation

Developing uniform implementation guidelines for the assessment plan is essential for insuring that it will be used. Because of the largely qualitative nature of the information gathered, it is often the impression that the methods used for collecting and reporting children's personal performance data are unstructured. Therefore, while the specific information gathered on each child may be different, the procedure for gathering it should be a standardized. To assist in developing this procedure, a number of things should be considered.

When Should the Information Be Collected? In order to assess developmental change in children, baseline information is essential. This information must be gathered early in the school year, but if gathered too early, those collecting and reporting the information might not be familiar enough with individual children to make valid observations. Therefore, a time early enough in the year to establish baseline, but late enough after the start of school to insure valid observational information, is most beneficial for a first-time observation.

Another issue related to the timing of information collection is curriculum related. If one is interested in evaluating the effectiveness of a particular curriculum experience, it might be important to gather information on all of the children following a specific unit or activity.

How Often Should the Information Be Collected? In order to assess progress, the spacing of the collection points must be far enough apart to allow development to happen, but not so far apart that something developmentally important that might occur between the collection points is missed. If there are too few collection points, the information will not be as useful for assessing individual children and for modifying the curriculum. If there are too many collection points, the task of assessment becomes to cumbersome and the volume of information collected becomes too great. While the timing of collection points may depend on individual children or individual types of behaviors observed, a common schedule should be drawn for assessing those things designated as critical for reporting progress.

What Types of Information Should Be Collected? In an alternative assessment plan it is important to designate what types of information will be collected. This information should vary according to the types of knowledge, skills, values, and attitudes that are emphasized in the activities and content areas addressed by the curriculum. Process-oriented as well as product-oriented information should be made part of each child's assessment plan. As stated earlier, both teacher-selected and child-selected material should be included. According to Tierney, Carter, and Desai (1991), involving children in a cooperative assessment process both motivates children and raises their self-esteem.

Who Will Collect the Information? An alternative assessment program should include multiple sources of information. As such, teachers' descriptions of children's behaviors only represent one of many avenues used to collect information. In addition to teachers, parents, area specialists, as well as the children themselves should be considered viable sources. Both formal (e.g., tests, standardized assessments) as well as informal information sources should be included.

What Format Will Be Used for Reporting the Information? Deciding to whom the information will go and for what purpose it will be used are necessary prerequisites for determining the format. A summary progress report in the form of a checklist may be appropriate for parents, but a teacher may need more detailed anecdotal records to determine how the curriculum should be modified to meet the child's developmental needs. Whatever the format, the information should be meaningful, useful, and not overwhelming.

Develop a Plan for Using the Assessment Information

The assessment committee should consider the ways assessment information will be utilized. These could include:

1. Curriculum planning—to develop curriculum activities as well as to modify the curriculum to meet the needs of individual children.
2. Measuring pupil progress—to measure the rate at which individual children are progressing through the curriculum areas as well as the degree to which children are able to effectively use the knowledge they've constructed and/or acquired.
3. Measuring curriculum effectiveness—to measure the curric-

ular activities' validity in achieving their stated goals/objectives with individuals or groups of children.

4. Reporting information to parents—to provide concrete evidence to parents regarding their child's progress. (A method for reducing the information to a reasonable and meaningful amount should be the major goal of this aspect of the assessment plan.)

CONCLUSION

What should be evident from the information and ideas presented in this chapter is that assessment flows out of, and in fact, becomes integrated within the curriculum. Assessment should serve the teacher and the learner by being sensitive to the individual manner in which children learn and develop, and by being the driving force in modifying the curriculum to meet individual children's needs.

In order to illustrate the processes described in this chapter, a case study is presented in appendix B documenting one school's development of an alternative assessment program. While a stated goal of alternative assessment procedures is to be sensitive to individual differences in children, a parallel to this is that an alternative assessment program and implementation strategy is also sensitive to the unique characteristics and needs of the school that develops it. As such, the case study presented here is only a model for plan development, and its particular components should not be used as a model for developing an assessment program in another setting. What should be noted is the link between evaluation and curriculum and the continuity among the assessment pieces.

As stated above, one of the advantages of using an alternative assessment approach is that it doesn't disrupt the process of curriculum implementation. The many developmental and learning activity areas in the early childhood classroom afford teachers many opportunities to engage in assessment and evaluation. In chapter 9, suggestions are given related to what types of developmental and learning activities might be assessed within various early education classroom contexts.

Integrating Alternative Assessment Procedures Into the Early Childhood Curriculum

It is often stated that the curriculum in early childhood education should be integrated (Gullo, 1992). According to Krogh (1990), in an integrated curriculum each of the component parts is recognized, in and of itself, for its significance, but each of the components is also recognized as part of a significant whole, and as such, is incorporated into the whole. The adoption of a curriculum philosophy that includes integration generally means that the curriculum is viewed, either consciously or unconsciously, in a holistic manner.

What exactly are the component parts that become integrated in this approach to curriculum? The component parts of the curriculum can be viewed in different ways. They may be the content areas such as math, social studies, reading/writing/language, and science. They may also be related to implementation of the curriculum as in, for example, the way activities, physical environment, materials, and teacher/child interaction are components of the curriculum. One final way of considering what the component parts of curriculum might look like would be to consider what goes into early childhood program development. In this more macro-view, the components of early childhood programming might be considered to be curriculum goals and objectives, curriculum development, curriculum implementation, and curriculum and individual evaluation.

This final position will be the focus of this chapter. In the following sections, several areas of developmental and learning activity within the early childhood classroom will be discussed and strategies for integrating alternative assessment into these areas will be described. No attempt will be made to generate possible learning outcomes, rather the focus will be a discussion about general academic and developmental characteristics that might be evident.

ART ACTIVITIES

Children engaged in art or art-like activities can convey much information concerning their development and their academic skills. Lowenfeld and Brittain (1975) have identified six developmental stages in children's drawings. They are reminiscent of children's levels of cognitive development. The six stages that have been identified along with their approximates age-level expectancies are:

1. Random scribbling (1–2½ years old)
2. Controlled scribbling (2½–3½ years old)
3. Naming of scribbling (3½–4 years old)
4. Representation attempts (4–5 years old)
5. Preschematic drawing (5–7 years old) and
6. Schematic stage (7–9 years old).

These stages of drawing development disclose a number of things about the children. Their conceptualization of the world around them is often represented through their artwork. Their use of form, perspective taking, and color are all mirrored in their art. And, less obviously, children's representational thinking ability and understanding of part-whole relationships are also reflected.

From a more purely maturational perspective, one can tell much about children's fine motor ability from their artwork. Their ability to grasp, to make steady, controlled marks, and to make coordinated figures are all areas that can be informally evaluated in the art area. Examples of their artwork are often included in children's portfolios as evidence of developmental progress. They like to talk about their artwork, which provides teachers with a good opportunity to observe spontaneous language ability.

BLOCK ACTIVITIES

It is unfortunate that the use of blocks in the early childhood curriculum is seldom extended past kindergarten. Children learn much by using blocks, and teachers learn much about children by observing them use the blocks. Children demonstrate a number of conceptual skills in their use of blocks including the following:

- Classification—using blocks of similar sizes and shapes for building a structure, for sorting the blocks in cooperative building, and for putting the blocks away on shelves.
- Concepts—understanding or lack of understanding of size, shape, equivalency, one-to-one correspondence, seriation, measurement, and number.
- Language—expressing the names of the shapes and sizes and describing their constructions as they build using both attributional and functional vocabulary.
- Sensorimotor—demonstrating balance, fine-motor manipulation of objects, and perspective taking; understanding figure-ground relationships and part-whole relationships.
- Problem solving—negotiating with others, conserving, establishing equivalent sets using non-equivalent sizes of blocks, making storage decisions, and constructing geometric figures.

DRAMATIC PLAY ACTIVITIES

Dramatic play can occur in a number of different classroom areas. The housekeeping corner of the room is most often associated with dramatic play. In addition, the puppet stage area and at times the rug and outside areas also facilitate dramatic play in young children. Dramatic play is rich in information regarding developmental and academic accomplishments.

Language Development

Many insights about children's language development can be learned from observing them in dramatic play situations. Technical aspects of their language production, such as sentence structure and phonological development, become evident during spontaneous dramatic play. During dramatic play children may be less inhibited and therefore more likely to demonstrate their language capabilities. And the words children use in their spontaneous language during dramatic play is a good indication of the kinds of vocabulary skills they possess.

Social and Emotional Development

Dramatic play gives teachers an opportunity to evaluate children's abilities to relate to other children. Dramatic play situations often include some amount of cooperation and role play, and through these elements it is possible to determine particular aspects of the child's social development. Children often assume the role of others, such as fathers, mothers, teachers, community helpers, or other children. Through these actions, it is possible to assess children's perceptions of others' social roles.

During dramatic play children's emotions may surface. Through the role play children often allow their fear, anger, joy, apprehension, excitement, or frustration to emerge during the themes that are played out. In early childhood education it is particularly important to understand how these emotions affect the day-to-day lives of children, including how they affect behavior in early education settings.

Concept and Skill Development

Dramatic play provides a non-threatening vehicle that children can use to practice the skills and concepts they are acquiring. Through focused observation of children during these situations, teachers often can determine the extent to which the children have mastered the particular skills and concepts that are the focus of the curriculum objectives.

SCIENCE AND DISCOVERY ACTIVITIES

The science and discovery area in the early childhood classroom provides the principle location where teachers can observe children processing information, constructing new knowledge, reconstructing existing knowledge, and solving problems. Through the kinds of activities that occur in the science and discovery area, children's understanding of many early scientific principles can be evaluated. It should be noted that sand and water activity could also be included here.

Children's understanding of the process of transformation is one of the scientific principles that can be assessed. Do children understand whether or not a transformation is relevant? This is the primary requisite to the development of conservation concepts. A transformation is relevant if something has been added or subtracted from the original quantity. If the quantity has been changed perceptually, but nothing has been added to or taken from the quantity, the transformation is irrelevant. This understanding is important for certain problem solving tasks.

Children's metacognitive ability can be assessed during science and discovery activities. Metacognition is awareness of one's own lack of understanding (Markman, 1977), not an easy task for the preoperational child who exhibits egocentric tendencies. Yet, this is an important ability to possess in order to progress cognitively.

Children's divergent thinking abilities can also be assessed through science activities. Divergent thinking refers to the ability to come up with multiple strategies for solving problems (Clements & Gullo, 1984). By observing children actively engaged in scientific activity, it is possible to determine the creativity that children use in their approach to problem solving situations.

Teachers can learn much about children's attributional knowledge by observing them during discovery activities. Attributional knowledge means children's understanding of the characteristics of objects and how those properties affect their function. As teachers watch how children use and categorize objects spontaneously, children's understanding of object attribute becomes more obvious.

Finally, in addition to observing and assessing those general cognitive abilities discussed above, teachers can also observe and assess for children's understanding of specific knowledge. For example, if the class is engaged in a science unit on magnets, can children develop rules for what kinds of objects magnets can and cannot attract? In a unit on floating and sinking, can the children successfully categorize objects according to whether they can sink or float?

MATH AND MANIPULATIVE ACTIVITY AREAS

Activities in the classroom's math and manipulative areas can also be very informative regarding children's problem solving skills. By manipulating different types of objects such as unifix cubes, pattern blocks, puzzles, and dice, children indicate their ability to sustain patterns, seriate (put objects in order), form geometric shapes, and perform mathematical operations.

In addition, there are also specialized mathematically oriented materials that may be available in some classrooms. As children manipulate cuisenaire rods, for example, teachers can observe their ability to estimate, demonstrate fractional relationships, and understand place value (Cruikshank, 1992). By having opportunities to watch children manipulate Dienes Multibase Arithmetic Blocks, teachers will have a better basis for evaluating children's understanding of place value, regrouping, addition, and subtraction (Goldberg, 1992).

By observing children using puzzles, teachers can learn about children's understanding of part-whole relationships. Children's visual discrimination of form may also be assessed to some extent.

Finally, children's fine motor abilities may be ascertained by observing their activity at the manipulative or math areas. By discerning this, a teacher would be better able to make decisions regarding what type of objects are best suited for an individual child.

LANGUAGE, LISTENING, READING, AND WRITING ACTIVITIES

Today, early childhood education practitioners, consider language, listening, reading, and writing to be integrated skills and developmental processes, and usually label them literacy. Obviously teachers can tell much about children's language by noting their behavior in the literacy areas of the classroom. In addition, teachers need only observe children in the process of communication, either oral or written, to determine what they know about the process of reading and writing. Evaluating children's reading and writing skills, such as sound-letter correspondence, sound analysis, decoding, spelling, listening, and comprehension, are all possible by observing children in the literacy areas.

During literature time teachers have opportunities to assess children's capacity to tell or retell stories by focusing on their capability to sequence events, recall details, demonstrate comprehension, and provide sufficient information so that others can understand the story. As children get older, similar capacities can be assessed by appraising children's writing.

EPILOGUE

Making decisions! Making decisions is one of the primary things that early childhood professionals do. They make decisions related to curriculum content and to curriculum implementation strategies. They make decisions related to which practice is best suited for which purpose and for which child. Most of the information that teachers base their decision-making on is provided by the children themselves.

Assessment and evaluation are useful tools that can help collect, organize, and make sense out of the information that early childhood professionals gather about children and the curriculum. In a sense, all competent teachers are early childhood researchers: collecting data, generating knowledge, and defining and re-defining practice based upon the information collected and the knowledge generated. Understanding assessment and evaluation, as well as the potential implications for their use, is the basis for making sound decisions. However, it is widely known in research that one can use the data in different ways, even to justify inappropriate practices. It is hoped that this book has shed some light on the role of assessment and evaluation in early childhood education in such a way as to enable practitioners to use the information they gather to make valid decisions about the status and future of the children in their charge. The decisions they make based upon this information greatly affect how children learn and how they live. Ultimately, there are few decisions of greater import to be made.

"The children we teach best are those who need us least." This concluding statement from the Preface is too often true and one based upon practice that is grounded in assessment. It is hoped that

101

after reading this book, we can better use assessment and evaluation information to help us teach all children best, whether they
need us the most or the least.

A Glossary of Assessment Instruments in Early Childhood Education

In this appendix, a number of assessments will be described. The instruments will be categorized according to the following: (a) developmental screening instruments; (b) readiness/achievement tests; and (c) diagnostic instruments. This is not meant to be an exhaustive list of instruments found in the field nor is it meant to be an endorsement. The choice of instruments found in this appendix represent those that are the most likely to be used or encountered by early childhood educators.

DEVELOPMENTAL SCREENING TESTS

Denver Developmental Screening Test (DDST: Frankenburg, Dodds, Fandal, Kazuk, & Cohrs, 1975). The DDST is an individually administered screening instrument. It is to be used with children between the ages of birth to 6 years old. The following developmental areas are assessed: (a) language; (b) fine motor; (c) gross motor; and (d) personal-social. The test is norm-referenced and score outcomes include delay, abnormal, untestable, and normal. No special training is required to administer the test.

Developmental Indicators for Assessment of Learning (Revised) (DIAL-R: Mardell-Czudnowski & Goldenberg, 1983). The DIAL-R is an individually administered screening instrument. It is meant to be used with children between the ages of 2 and 6 years old. The following developmental areas are assessed: (a) motor skills; (b) conceptual skills; and (c) language skills. Scaled scores are derived for each of the subtests as well as for the total score. The scaled scores can be compared with cutoffs scored to identify children in further need of diagnostic assessment. The test can potentially identify children who are at-risk for academic failure as well as those who are academically precocious.

Early Screening Inventory (ESI: Meisels & Wiske, 1983). The ESI is an individually administered, norm-referenced screening test. It can be used with children between the ages of 4 and 6 years old. The following developmental areas are assessed: (a) expressive and receptive language; (b) auditory reception; (c) gross and fine motor; (d) reasoning; (e) perceptual-motor; and (f) general behavior. The normed scores are provided by age. The total score is converted to "ok," "unscreen," or "refer." The instrument can be administered by teachers or other educators.

The McCarthy Screening Test (MST: McCarthy, 1980). The MST is an individually administered test which is made up of six of the 18 subtests of the McCarthy Scales of Children's Abilities. The following areas are assessed: (a) right-left orientation; (b) verbal memory; (c) draw-a-design; (d) numerical memory; (e) conceptual grouping; and (e) leg coordination. The scores are norm referenced by age. The test can be used with children between the ages of 4 and 6 1/2 years old.

Minnesota Child Development Inventory (MCDI: Ireton & Thwing, 1974) The MCDI is a parent questionnaire consisting of 320 questions that can be answered by "yes" or "no." The questions are designed to be appropriated for children between the ages of 3 and 6 years old. The following areas are assessed: (a) gross and fine motor; (b) expressive language; (c) conceptual comprehension; (d) situational comprehension; (e) self-help; (f) personal-social; and (g) general development. For each of the areas listed, children's derived scores are compared to age scores and the percentage below expectancy is noted.

Minneapolis Preschool Screening Instrument (MPSI: Lichtenstein, 1982). The MPSI is an individually administered, norm-referenced screening instrument, designed to be used with children between the ages of 3 years, 7 months and 5 years, 4 months. The 11 subtests included are: (a) building; (b) copying shapes; (c) providing information; (d) matching shapes; (e) completing sentences; (f) hopping/balancing; (g) naming colors; (h) counting; (i) using prepositions; (j) identifying body parts; and (k) sentence repetition. The test can be administered by teachers and seems to be a good predictor of learning difficulties for at least one year following the administration of the test.

READINESS/ACHIEVEMENT TESTS

Boehm Test of Basic Concepts (Boehm, 1986). The Boehm Test is an individually or group administered instrument. It was designed to be used with children between the ages of 3 and 5 years old. The test can be administered by teachers and assesses children's understanding of the following concepts; (a) size; (b) direction; (c) spacial relationships; and (d) quantity. The information derived from the test's scores can be used by the teacher as a guide for curriculum planning. It has also been viewed as a good measure of school readiness.

The Brigance Diagnostic Inventory of Early Development (Brigance, 1978). The Brigance is an individually administered, criterion-referenced screening instrument. It can be used with children between the ages of birth and 7 years old. The following areas are assessed: (a) gross and fine motor skills; (b) self-help skills; (c) language development; (d) general knowledge; (e) reading readiness; and (f) math and writing skills. The test can be administered by teachers and the results can be used to identify strengths and weaknesses in children for the purposes of developing instructional objectives.

California Achievement Test (CAT: CTB/McGraw Hill 1985). The CAT is a group administered, norm-referenced test. The intended purpose of the test is to provide information for making educational decisions regarding improved instruction in the basic skills. The following academic areas are assessed: (a) prereading/reading; (b) spelling; (c) language; (d) mathematics; and (e) reference skills.

Circus (Anderson & Bogatz, 1976). Circus is a group administered test appropriately used with children between the ages of 3 1/2 and 7 years old. The instrument assesses the following areas thought to be important for early success in school: (a) language/reading; (b) perceptual development; (c) mathematical knowledge; (d) processing information; (e) divergent thinking; (f) and attitudes/interests. The test can be used by teachers and teachers' aides. The results are meant to assist educators to identify the educational needs of children.

Cognitive Skills Assessment Battery (CSAB: Boehm & Slater, 1981). The CSAB is a criterion-referenced assessment instrument. It was designed to be used with children in prekindergarten and kindergarten. It can be given by teachers in the beginning of the school year to assist in curriculum planning. The CSAB assesses: (a) the child's environment; (b) discrimination of similarities and differences; (c) comprehension; (d) concept formation; (e) coordination; and (f) memory.

Cooperative Preschool Inventory—Revised (CPI: Caldwell, 1970). The CPI is an individually administered screening instrument. It is standardized and can be given by a teacher or trained paraprofessional. It can be used with children between the ages of 3 and 6 years old. The following academic areas are assessed: (a) independence and self-help; (b) following directions; (c) basic concepts; (d) visual motor; and (e) basic information and vocabulary. There are two stated goals for the test. The first goal is to assess individual children's achievement levels in the areas thought to be indicative of school success. The second goal is to identify areas of deficits in children from homes of economic poverty in order to reduce or eliminate these areas.

Gesell School Readiness Test (Gesell Institute of Human Development, 1978). The Gesell is an academic screening instrument intended for use with children at the prekindergarten and kindergarten levels. Its stated purpose is to identify children who are ready to begin kindergarten. In addition, it also states that it answers questions related to appropriate grade placement.

Metropolitan Readiness Test (MRT: Nurss & McGauvran, 1976). The MRT is a group administered readiness test. Level I is appropriate for children in preschool and kindergarten; Level II is appropriate for children in kindergarten to first grade. The MRT assesses important underlying skills important for early learning. The Level I MRT assesses skills in the following areas: (a) auditory memory; (b) rhyming; (c) beginning consonants; (d) letter recognition; (e) visual matching; (f) school language and listening; and (g) quantitative knowledge.

The Level II MRT assesses: (a) understanding beginning consonants; (b) auditory memory; (c) letter recognition; (d) visual matching; (e) finding patterns; (f) school language and listening; (g) quantitative concepts; and (h) quantitative operations.

The MRT can be administered by the teacher. Content referenced information is provided in the manual for curriculum and instruction planning.

Preschool Screening System (PSS: Hainsworth & Hainsworth, 1974). The PSS is designed to be individually administered to children between the ages of 4 years, 4 months and 5 years, 4 months. The screening system when combined with the accompanying parent questionnaire can be used to better meet individual children's needs through curriculum development. The PSS gives a quick indication of learning skills, including: (a) language skills; (b) visual motor skills; and (c) gross motor skills. The parent questionnaire provides information regarding children's home behavior, medical history and developmental information.

Stanford Early School Achievement Test (Madden, Gardner, & Collins, 1984). The Stanford Early Achievement Test is a group test designed to measure cognitive abilities in young children. Level I is designed to be administered to children before entering kindergarten. Level II is designed for children at the end of kindergarten and the beginning of first grade. Areas assessed are: (a) sounds and letters; (b) reading words; (c) listening to words and stories; (d) math; and (e) environment of the child. According to the test manual, the results provide information regarding an individual's cognitive development as a baseline for instructional planning. The test is norm referenced and can be administered by the teacher.

DIAGNOSTIC TESTS

Battelle Developmental Inventory (BDI: Newborg, Stock, Wnek, Guidubaldi, & Sninicki, 1984). The BDI is both a norm- and criterion-referenced diagnostic instrument. It is an appropriate test for children between the ages of birth to 8 years old. The following domains are assessed: (a) personal-social—ability to engage in meaningful interactions; (b) language/communication—receptive and expressive language ability; (c) cognitive—perceptual discrimination, memory, reasoning ability, and academic skills; (d) adaptive—ability to become independent, and (e) motor development—fine and gross motor skills. The test must be administered by trained individuals. The BDI also includes instructions for administration to children with physical handicaps.

Bayley Scales of Infant Development (Bayley, 1969). The Bayley is an individual assessment appropriate to measure the developmental progress of children between the ages of birth and 2 1/2 years old. It contains both a Mental Scale and a Motor Scale. The Mental Scale assesses: (a) sensory and perceptual acuity/discrimination; (b) object permanence and memory; (c) vocalization and communication; and (d) early generalization and classification abilities. The Motor Scale measures: (a) body control; and (b) small and large muscle coordination. Administration is by a highly trained individual.

Gesell Developmental Schedules—Revised (Knoblock, Stevens & Malone, 1987). The Gesell Developmental is a norm-referenced diagnostic instrument designed for infants between the ages of 4 and 36 months. The purpose of the assessment is to diagnose the mental ability of infants in five areas: (a) adaptive behavior; (b) gross motor; (c) fine motor; (d) language development; and (e) personal/social development.

Home Inventory (Caldwell, 1972). The Home Scale is appropriate for use for children during the preschool years, including kindergarten. It is designed for use in research to assess the quality of the home environment. This is accomplished through observation in a number of areas: (a) responsivity of the mother to the child—verbal and emotional; (b) environmental organization—physical and temporal; and (c) stimulation of the child using books, games, and other toys.

Kaufman Assessment Battery for Children (KABC: Kaufman & Kaufman, 1983). The KABC is a norm-referenced intelligence and achievement test. It is individually administered and appropriate for children between 2 and 15 years of age. The test is divided into three areas: (a) sequential processing; (b) simultaneous processing; and (c) achievement. The sequential processing subtests include hand movements, number recall, and word order. The simultaneous processing includes magic window, face recognition, Gestalt closure, triangles, matrix analogies, spacial memory, and photo series. The achievement subtests include expressive vocabulary, faces and places, math, riddles, reading/decoding, and reading/understanding. Both subtest and global score are derived. The KABC was designed for use in both clinical and academic settings.

McCarthy Scales of Children's Abilities (MSCA: McCarthy, 1972). The MSCA is an individually administered, norm-referenced assessment instrument. It was designed for use with children between the ages of 2 1/2 and 8 1/2 years. It consists of 18 separate subtests, the scores of which are combined to assess six developmental domains. (a) verbal; (b) perceptual-performance; (c) quantitative; (d) general cognitive; (e) memory; and (f) motor. The test can be used to diagnose children with learning difficulties or other exceptional conditions.

Peabody Picture Vocabulary Test—Revised (PPVT: Dunn & Dunn, 1981). The PPVT is an individually administered, norm-referenced test. It is designed for children 2 1/2 years of age and older. It measures children's receptive vocabulary ability. Two alternative forms of the PPVT are available for test-retest purposes. Scores are provided in the form of standard scores, percentiles, age scores, and stanine scores. It is not intended for use as a substitute measure of cognitive functioning. This is especially true for children with disabilities.

Stanford-Binet Intelligence Scale—Fourth Edition (Thorndike, Hagen, & Sattler, 1986). The Stanford-Binet is a norm-referenced, individually administered test of overall intelligence or cognitive functioning. It is designed for use with individuals from 2 years of age to adults. The four general areas assessed by the test include: (a) verbal reasoning; (b) abstract/visual reasoning; (c) quantitative reasoning; and (d) short-term memory. The scores from 15 subtests are combined to yield performance scores in each of the four areas listed above. Nonverbal reasoning and verbal comprehension best characterize the test for children between the ages of 2 and 6. Standard scores can be derived for each of the subtests as well as an overall IQ score. In order to administer the test or interpret the findings, extensive training in psychometric and psychological procedures is required.

Vineland Social Maturity Scale (Sparrow, Balla, & Cicchetti, 1984). The Vineland is a criterion-referenced test appropriate for individuals from birth to adulthood. It was designed to assess an individual's social capacity for self-care and independent living. The following areas are assessed: (a) self-help; (b) self-direction; (c) occupation; (d) communication; (e) locomotion; and (f) general socialization skills. The information is gathered through interview.

Wechsler Preschool and Primary Scale of Intelligence—Revised (WPPSI-R: Wechsler, 1989). The WPPSI-R is a norm-referenced intelligence test designed for use with children between the ages of 3 to 7 years old. The test includes a verbal scale (information, comprehension, arithmetic, vocabulary, similarities, sentences) and a performance scale (object assembly, geometric design, block design, mazes, picture completion, animal pegs). The test yields a Verbal IQ, Performance IQ, and a Full Scale IQ (includes both the verbal and performance IQs). Special training to administer the test is required in addition to a background in psychometric assessment procedures and knowledge of the effects of culture on performance.

Case Study: One School's Attempt at Developing an Alternative Assessment Program

Garfield Elementary School is located in Milwaukee, Wisconsin, and is part of the Milwaukee Public School system. As one of the city's specialty schools, Garfield focuses on early childhood education and math-science education. Its curriculum addresses children's needs beginning at age 3 and continues through the fifth grade. Children become involved in planning their learning, carrying out the activities that are planned, and reviewing their work during various phases of completion. The activities include both product and process and the curriculum is based upon learner abilities rather than on specific content. The six learner abilities that form the basis for the curriculum at Garfield Elementary are as follows:

1. *Communicative ability*—collecting, processing, and relaying ideas and thoughts through various means of expression, including oral language, reading, writing, and technology.
2. *Cognitive ability*—making sense out of the world through reasoning, problem solving, and decision making.
3. *Physical ability*—constructing knowledge through motor movement. Additional emphases are placed on children's development of awareness of the world through their senses, physical fitness, and stress management techniques.
4. *Creative ability*—utilizing past experiences and ideas to create something unique and original. Divergent thinking is of primary concern.

5. *Social/emotional ability*—developing appropriate social and emotional attitudes and responses to other individuals and to events through both intra- and interpersonal relationships.
6. *Citizenship ability*—displaying appropriate attitudes and responses through active participation in the community. Additional foci within the curriculum are on environment and global issues.

During the summer of 1990, a group of teachers and parents from Garfield Elementary School met to discuss their beliefs and philosophy regarding assessment and young children (Zagorski, 1991). The teachers and other staff members reviewed the literature on assessment and came to agree on a set of beliefs about assessment. During the fall of the 1990–1991 school year, the entire staff of Garfield school endorsed and drew up an assessment plan based upon these beliefs (Zagorski, 1991). The plan stated

1. School is designed to teach students how to be productive, satisfied life-long learners.
2. The teacher's role is to develop the six learner abilities (listed above). Teachers are both teachers and learners, just as the students are teachers and learners as well.
3. A successful student is a student who makes progress in the six learner abilities. Each student will demonstrate varying levels of competence in each area. Progress is what is important!
4. Learners have multiple abilities that are demonstrated in multiple formats and must be assessed in multiple ways.
5. Assessment is on-going and is designed to check in different ways whether the student is progressing in competence in the six areas.
6. Assessment focuses on the student, not the content, and is designed to help teachers, parents, and students themselves see the students' strengths and weaknesses.

Keeping consistent with both their beliefs about assessment and the six learner abilities that formed the basis for the curriculum at Garfield School, the teachers and staff of the school organized their alternative assessment program to focus on three forms (shown at the end of this case description): a checklist, a portfolio model, and a summative teacher report.

There are a number of characteristics of the checklist (see Figure B.1) that make it consistent with the teachers' and staff's philosophy regarding assessment. The behaviors listed on the checklist did not focus on specific content skills such as counting or letter recognition. Rather, the focus was on the broader developmental and achievement-oriented behaviors reflective of the six learner abilities. The belief in multiple learner abilities is reflected through the six learner abilities. The specific skills of multiple content areas are integrated into these abilities. Finally, the rating of the child using the checklist requires the teacher to rate change over time. This reflects both the progress orientation and the on-going nature of the school's philosophy regarding evaluation.

In designing the structure of the portfolio (see Figure B.2) the teachers also looked to their philosophy and curriculum. The structure of the portfolio is therefore not arranged around content areas. Rather, the evidence collected for the portfolios is organized around abilities and, to be consistent with the belief that evaluation is on-going and measures progress, evidence is arranged chronologically. In addition to children's original work, the portfolios also contain different forms of ability rating that reflect requirements of the school system or of the school.

The activity summary sheets (see Figure B.3) and the report of student progress (report card; see Figure B.4) were derived from the other two alternative assessment forms that were developed. The activity summary sheet was used by the teacher to describe the reasons for including a piece of evidence in the child's portfolio. Figures B.5 and B.6 are examples of the front and back of progress report envelopes that are also used as assessment opportunities. It should be noted that children and their parents are involved in the progress report process

Finally, under the school's curriculum and assessment philosophy. Garfield's staff developed a series of "Abilities-Based Assessment" activities. The purpose of these activities was to provide teachers with examples of integrated lessons that could be used to assess the various learner abilities addressed in the curriculum. Figure B.7 shows examples of these activities at various developmental levels represented at the school.

Figure B.1. Garfield abilities checklist.

GARFIELD ABILITIES CHECKLIST

Little Progress
Some Progress
Good Progress

COMMUNICATIONS

	Sept.	Jan.	May

Speaking: Children will demonstrate the ability to:
- Ask questions and answer questions of others.
- Put facts and understandings in their own words.
- Use language to solve problems.
- Participate in a variety of oral language activities.
- Make and use recordings of spoken language using audiovisual technology.
- Share thoughts and understanding with an attentive audience.
- State and support opinions.

Listening: Children will demonstrate the ability to:
- Comprehend a message.
- Provide appropriate feedback.
- Attend to the speaker and the message.
- Respect the speaker and the message.
- Recognize purposes for listening.
- Evaluate the message.
- Question when the meaning is unclear.

Writing: Children will demonstrate the ability to:
- Write using its various forms.
- Use a variety of writing tools and equipment.
- Express written thoughts on self-selected topics.
- Write across the curriculum.
- Observe and demonstrate the connecting of spoken and written language.
- Acquire and extend writing skills.
- Publish selected compositions.

Reading: Children will demonstrate the ability to:
- Read varied genre of children's literature.
- Read own compositions.
- Read across the curriculum.
- Acquire reading skills at appropriate levels.

COGNITIVE

	Sept.	Jan.	May

Problem Solving: Children will demonstrate the ability to:
- Make choices independently.
- Make plans and recognize alternatives.
- Elaborate ideas.
- Use multiple strategies to solve problems.
- Use resources to solve problems.
- Understand that there is more than one way to solve a problem.
- Question and challenge.

Logical: Children will demonstrate the ability to:
- Classify and order objects.
- Compare and contrast objects.
- Organize information.
- Form concepts.
- Draw conclusions.
- Analyze concepts.
- Synthesize ideas.
- Estimate.

Memory: Children will demonstrate the ability to:
- Recall past events and experiences.
- Link the past and the present.
- Apply the past to the present and future.

Attention: Children will demonstrate the ability to:
- Attend to self selected tasks.
- Attend to activities chosen by others.
- Ignore distractions.

Curiosity: Children will demonstrate the ability to:
- Be curious about the environment.
- Exhibit a love of learning.
- Inquire about new things.
- Show interest in ideas.
- Use imagination.

Perception: Children will demonstrate the ability to:
- Gain information through the senses.

(Figure continues on page 116)

Figure B.1 (cont'd.)

CREATIVE/AESTHETIC	Sept.	Jan.	May

Create: Children will demonstrate the ability to:
- Explore ideas.
- Express own unique perspective using materials, sounds, or movement.
- Use recognized methods to produce original works.

Respond: Children will demonstrate the ability to:
- Appreciate the artistic expressions of others.
- Appreciate the diversity of expression from others.

Evaluate: Children will demonstrate the ability to:
- Develop preferences.
- Give reasons for preferences.
- Recognize artistic contributions of diverse cultures.

PHYSICAL

Children will demonstrate the ability to:
- Perform locomotor skills.
- Show fine motor coordination.
- Use motor skills for personally meaningful purposes.
- Exhibit healthy living practices.

SOCIAL/EMOTIONAL

Children will demonstrate the ability to:
- Initiate independent activities.
- Act independently.
- Participate in group activities.
- Complete assigned tasks.
- Express emotions verbally and nonverbally.
- Use language to deal with conflict.
- Take another's perspective.
- Exhibit a sense of fairness.
- Cooperate with others.
- Negotiate with others.

CITIZENSHIP

Children will demonstrate the ability to:
- Be aware of the world around.
- Exhibit sportsmanship.
- Cooperate with teachers.
- Cooperate with others.
- Respect materials.

Figure B.2. Garfield elementary student portfolio cover sheet
(April 1991 version).

Required Data

The following is a list of the required data that must be kept in each student
portfolio.

1. Three writing samples (Oct., Jan., and May).
2. Three reading verifications.
3. Two oral language samples (Sept. and May).
4. Abilities checklist.
5. Whole Language Behavior Inventory.
6. Journal entries.
7. Andecdotal records/observations.

Pertinent Data

The following is a list of pertinent data that should be kept for each student
throughout the school year.

1. Parent conference notes.
2. Social/Emotional Checklist (K3, K4).
3. Any interest inventories, reading lists, etc.

Supporting Data

The following is a list of suggestions for collecting supporting evidence that may
be included in the portfolio. For your convenience, the captioned summary
sheet should be attached to any piece of evidence.

Communications: Audio tapes, video tapes, writing samples, journal
entries, projects, logs, dictated stories.

Cognitive: Photos of projects, solutions to problems, lab work samples of
story problems, journal entries.

Social/Emotional: Anecdotal records, self-portraits.

Citizenship: Anecdotal records, projects, letters.

Physical Ability: Anecdotal records, observations, physical fitness tests,
video tapes.

Creative Ability: Projects, experiments, journal entries, writing samples,
audio and video tapes, photos, innovative solutions or approaches to
situations.

Please note: These lists are meant as suggestions. They are in no way meant to
limit you as a teacher. Hopefully, some of these selections will be made by
you and some by the students.

Figure B.3. Garfield activity summary sheet.

<u>**Garfield Caption Summary Sheet**</u>
April 1991 version

Child's Name: _____ Date: _____

Brief description of activity/project:

Reasons for selection:

What ability or abilities does this demonstrate?

Please attach any evidence to be included in portfolio.

Figure B.4. Student progress report.

 MILWAUKEE PUBLIC SCHOOLS

Garfield Avenue School
Report of Student Progress

Student's Name: _____ Grade: _____ School Year: 1992 - '93

Teacher: _____ Placement Next Term: _____

This Child: ↓	In class				In fine arts		In phys. ed.	

Attendance: Days Absent [ ][ ][ ] Times Tardy [ ][ ][ ]

Reading Level: At/Above / Below   1 2 3 4

Excellent Progress **G**ood Progress **S**ome Progress **N**ot Yet Progressing

This Child: ↓	In class				In fine arts		In phys. ed.	
	1	2	3	4	2	4	2	4
Cognitive Abilities								
Sets goals								
Persists in reaching goals								
Makes appropriate choices								
Uses alternatives in problem solving								
Follows the scientific method							*	*
Formulates questions								
Identifies problems								
Exhibits research skills							*	*
Collects and organizes information							*	*
Draws conclusions							*	*
Understands math concepts								
Communication Abilities								
Communicates ideas clearly in writing							*	*
Expresses ideas clearly when speaking								
Listens well								
Reads with fluency					*	*	*	*
Reads with understanding					*	*	*	*
Uses technology							*	*
Creative Abilities								
Develops projects							*	*
Uses imagination								
Transfers classroom lessons to real life situations								
Physical Abilities								
Develops fine motor skills								
Exhibits knowledge of healthful living								
Demonstrates physical coordination								
Social/Emotional Abilities								
Acts responsibly								
Respects others								
Participates in group projects								
Uses respectful language to deal with conflict								
Citizenship Abilities								
Exhibits sportsmanship								
Respects materials								
Cooperates with staff								
Cooperates with peers								
Exhibits respect for other cultures								

* Does not apply

(Figure continues on page 120)

Figure B.4 (cont'd.)

Garfield Avenue School
Report of Student Progress   School Year: 1992-'93

Student's Name: | Teacher:

LANGUAGE ARTS   2
☐1 -We have been learning:

SCIENCE
  -We have been exploring: 2
☐1

MATH
☐1 -We have been developing: 2

Figure B.4 (cont'd.)

Student's Name: _____

_____
                                                              Principal, Garfield Avenue School

SOCIAL STUDIES

[1] -We have been researching: [2]

_____

FINE ARTS

[1] -We have been learning: [2]

_____

HEALTH & PHYSICAL DEVELOPMENT
       -We have been developing: [2]
[1]

_____

ADDITIONAL COMMENTS

[1]   [2]

Figure B.5. Progress report envelope cover (front).

Garfield Avenue School
Progress Report

Student: _____

Teacher's
Signature: _____

Room: _____   Grade: _____

I'm proud because:

1st Report _____

_____

_____

2nd Report _____

_____

_____

3rd Report _____

_____

_____

Figure B.6. Progress report envelope cover (back).

My Goals

1st Report _____

_____

_____

_____

_____   _____
Child's Signature   Parent's Signature

2nd Report _____

_____

_____

_____

_____   _____
Child's Signature   Parent's Signature

3rd Report _____

_____

_____

_____

_____   _____
Child's Signature   Parent's Signature

Figure B.7. Ability-based assessment activities.

SURPRISE BOX (PRESCHOOL)

Brief Description of Activity   An object is placed in a large box that pertains to some topic being studied (letter of the alphabet, theme, color). The teacher gives a hint and the children respond by asking a question, such as, Is it something for a snack? Is it big? Is it heavy? Is it red? Students are encouraged to ask questions and use the answers to make conclusions.

Abilities Measured
Cognitive: Recognizes alternatives, elaborates ideas, uses imagination, draws conclusions, makes inferences
Communication: Clearly expresses ideas orally, listens with a purpose
Creative: Exhibits innovative thinking
Social/Emotional: Completes assigned task, takes turn

What Criteria or Standards Did You Use To Judge This?   Criteria included looking for children's questioning ability, which begins to develop in preschool. The teacher also looks for those children who never ask a question, so that they can be drawn out. Listening skills are also observed, as well as whether students understand the concepts being taught. Anecdotal records are one way of keeping track of the students progress.

ADOPT A TREE (K5)

Brief Description of Activity   The classes have adopted a tree in the neighborhood. Each month they observe their tree and record information on the attached sheet. They write their name and the month, and draw themselves and the tree. Each month's sheet is saved and put together in a book. Month to month progress is readily evident.

Abilities Measured
Cognitive: Recognizes alternatives, elaborates ideas, uses imagination
Communication: Expresses ideas clearly in a written form (drawing and writing), uses writing tools, writes in all content areas
Creative: Develops unique projects, expresses own unique perspective using materials, uses recognized methods to produce an original work
Social-Emotional: Initiates independent activity, completes assigned task, respects materials
Physical: Shows fine motor coordination

What Criteria or Standards Did You Use To Judge This? Criteria were determined by the teachers informally. They were looking for progress in the following areas:

1. Writing their names and months including letter formation, use of materials, use of details in picture
2. Draw conclusions and translate them into a drawing
3. Ability to see changes

WRITING SAMPLES (EMERGENT WRITERS/ EARLY FLUENCY–1ST GRADE)

Brief Description of Activity During the first month of school, the teacher chooses one of the child's writing samples and saves it. This very same sample is dictated to the child in the middle and at end of the year. These rewritings are then compared and contrasted with the original and with one another to determine progress. The comparison and discussions of changes in his/her writing ability can also be used to help the child be more aware of his/her progress in writing conventions and editing.

Abilities Measured

Cognitive: Sets goals, uses imagination
Communication: Expresses ideas clearly in written form, uses writing tools
Creative: Exhibits innovative thinking, expresses own unique perspective using
    materials, uses recognized methods to produce an original work
Social/Emotional: Initiates independent activity, completes assigned task,
    respects materials
Physical: Shows fine motor coordination

What Criteria or Standards Did You Use To Judge This? Criteria for judging this can be established by the teacher. Most readily adapted is a holistic scoring rubric.

SALT-DOUGH MAPS (GRADE 2)

Brief Description of Activity After completing a unit on landforms, directions, and map skills, the students constructed salt-dough maps. Before constructing the maps, the students made blueprints of what they were going to make. Then, using the salt-dough, they laid out the map and painted each landform appropriately, including a map key. Students then presented their maps and were videotaped talking about the landforms, etc.

(Figure continues on page 126)

Figure B.7 (cont'd.)

Abilities Measured

Cognitive: Sets goals, makes choices, uses alternatives in problem-solving, uses scientific tools, shows curiosity, uses basic math skills
Communication: Clearly expresses ideas orally
Creative: Develops unique projects, exhibits innovative thinking, develops fine motor skills, actively participates
Social/Emotional: Acts responsibly, respects others, participates in group projects, respects materials

What Criteria or Standards Did You Use To Judge This? Students were judged on the following criteria:

1. Did the map key coordinate with the map?
2. Could the child tell the class what was on the map?
3. Did the child form the landforms and bodies of water accurately?

SIMPLE MACHINES (GRADE 3)

Brief Description of Activity   Students have been studying simple machines in a science class. This is the culminating activity. Students create their own machine to do a job. Students are given the criteria for judging their projects in advance.

Abilities Measured

Cognitive: Sets goals, makes plans and recognizes alternatives, elaborates ideas, uses alternatives in problem-solving, uses scientific tools, uses basic math skills, demonstrates scientific method, uses imagination
Communication: Clearly expresses ideas orally
Creative: Develops unique projects, exhibits innovative thinking, expresses own unique perspective using materials, uses recognized methods to produce an original work
Social-Emotional: Initiates independent activity, completes assigned task, respects materials

What Criteria or Standards Did You Use To Judge This? Criteria is given to each child when the project is assigned. Students will be able to:

1. Identify the problem (the job to do)
2. Sketch (blueprint) and label the parts
3. List and get recyclable materials
4. Build the machine
5. Make changes if necessary
6. Present the project to the class with an understanding of simple machines

REFERENCES

American Psychological Association. (1974). *Standards for educational and psychological tests and manuals.* Washington, DC: Author.

Anastasiow, N. J. (1986). *Development and disability: A psychobiological analysis for special educators.* Baltimore: Brookes Publishing Co.

Anderson, S., & Bogatz, G. A. (1976). *Circus.* Princeton, NJ: Educational Testing Service.

Apgar, V. (1953). Proposal for a new method of evaluating the newborn infant. *Anesthesia and Analgesia, 52,* 260–267.

Apple M., & King, N. (1978). What do schools teach? In G. Willis (Ed.), *Qualitative education: Concepts and cases in curriculum criticism.* Berkeley, CA: McCutchan Publishing Co.

Bayley, N. (1969). *Bayley Scales of Infant Development.* Cleveland: The Psychological Corporation.

Bell, M. (1972). *A study of the readiness room program in a small school district in suburban Detroit, Michigan.* Unpublished doctoral dissertation, Wayne State University.

Blank, M., & Allen, D. (1976). Understanding "why." In M. Lewis (Ed.), *Origins of Intelligence.* New York: Plenum.

Boehm, A. E. (1986). *Boehm Test of Basic Concepts.* Cleveland: The Psychological Corporation.

Boehm, A. E. (1992). Glossary of assessment terms. In L. R Williams, & D. P. Fromberg (Eds.), *Encyclopedia of early childhood education.* New York: Garland Publishing, Inc.

Boehm, A. E., & Slater, B. (1981). *Cognitive Skills Assessment Battery.* New York: Teachers College Press.

Boehm, A. E., & Weinberg, R. A. (1987). *The classroom observer: Developing observation skills in early childhood settings.* New York: Teachers College Press.

Bredekamp, S. (1987). *Developmentally appropriate practice in early childhood programs serving children from birth through age 8.* Washington, DC: National Association for the Education of Young Children.

Brigance, A. (1978). *The Brigance Diagnostic Inventory of Early Development.* Curriculum Associate, Inc.

Bruner, J. S. (1966). *Towards a theory of instruction.* Cambridge, MA: Harvard University Press.

Cairns, H., & Hsu, J. R. (1978). Who, why, when, and how: A developmental study. *Journal of Child Language, 5,* 447–488.

Caldwell, B. (1970). *The Cooperative Preschool Inventory (Revised).* Reading, MA: Addison-Wesley.

Caldwell, B. (1972). *The Home Inventory.* Reading, MA: Addison-Wesley.

Cartwright, G. A., & Cartwright, G. P. (1984). *Developing observational skills.* New York: McGraw-Hill.

Chittenden, E. (1991). Authentic assessment, evaluation, and documentation of student performance. In V. Perrone (Ed.), *Expanding student assessment.* Alexandria, VA: Association for Supervision and Curriculum Development.

Clements, D. H., & Gullo, D. F. (1984). Effects of computer programming on young children's cognition. *Journal of Educational Psychology, 76,* 1051–1058.

Comer, J. (1980). *School power.* New York: Free Press.

Cruikshank, D. E. (1992). Cuisenaire rods. In L.R Williams & D.P. Fromberg (Eds.), *Encyclopedia of early childhood education.* New York: Garland Publishing, Inc.

Cryan, J. R. (1986). Evaluation: Plague or promise? *Childhood Education, 62,* 344–350.

CTB/McGraw-Hill (1985). *The California Achievement Test.* New York: McGraw-Hill.

Decker, C. A., & Decker, J. R. (1980). *Planning and administering early childhood programs.* Columbus, OH: Merrill Publishing Co.

Derman-Sparks, L. (1989). *Anti-bias curriculum: Tools for empowering young children.* Washington, DC: National Association for the Education of Young Children.

Dunn, L., & Dunn, L. (1981). *Peabody Picture Vocabulary Test—Revised.* Circle Pines, MN: American Guidance Service.

Durkin, D. (1987). Testing in the kindergarten. *The Reading Teacher, 40,* 766–770.

Frankenburg, W. F., Dodds, J., Fandal, A., Kazuk, E., & Cohrs, M. (1975). *Denver Developmental Screening Test.* Denver: Denver Developmental Materials.

Gardner, H. (1983). *Frames of mind: The theory of multiple intelligences.* New York: Basic Books.

Gesell Institute of Human Development (1978). *Gesell School Readiness Test.* Programs for Education.

Gnezda, M. T., & Bolig, R. (1988). *A national survey of public school testing of prekindergarten and kindergarten children.* Washington, DC: National Academy of Sciences.

Goldberg, L. (1992). Dienes multibase arithmetic blocks. In L. R Williams, & D. P. Fromberg (Eds.), *Encyclopedia of early childhood education.* New York: Garland Publishing, Inc.

Goodwin, W. R., & Driscoll, L. A. (1980). *Handbook for measurement and evaluation in early childhood education.* San Francisco: Jossey-Bass.

Gredler, G. R. (1984). Transition classes: A viable alternative for the at-risk child? *Psychology in the Schools, 21,* 463–470.

Gronlund, N. E. (1973). *Preparing criterion-referenced test for classroom instruction.* New York: Macmillan.

Gullo, D. F. (1981). Social class differences in preschool children's comprehension of wh-questions. *Child Development, 52, 736–740.*

Gullo, D. F. (1982). A developmental study of low- and middle-class children's responses to wh-questions. *First Language, 3, 211–221.*

Gullo, D. F. (1988, November). *Perspectives on controversial issues related to implementing the all-day kindergarten: Evaluation and assessment.* Paper presented at the Annual Meeting of the National Association for the Education of Young Children, Anaheim, CA.

Gullo, D. F. (1992). *Developmentally appropriate teaching in early childhood: Curriculum, implementation, evaluation.* Washington, DC: National Educational Association.

Gullo, D. F., & Ambrose, R. P. (1987). Perceived competence social acceptance in kindergarten: Its relationship to academic performance. *Journal of Educational Research, 8* (1), 28–32.

Gullo, D. F., Bersani, C., Clements, D. H., & Bayless, K. M. (1986). A comparative study of all-day, alternate-day, and half-day kindergarten schedules: Effects on achievement and classroom social behaviors. *Journal of Research in Childhood Education, 1* (2), 87–94.

Hainsworth, P. K., & Hainsworth, M. L. (1974). *Preschool Screening System.* Available from the authors at P.S.S., Box 1635, Pawtucket, RI 02862.

Harms, T., & Clifford, R. (1980). *The early childhood environment rating scale.* New York: Teachers College Press.

Inhelder, B., Sinclair, H., & Bovet, M. (1974). *Learning and the development of cognition.* Cambridge, MA: Harvard University Press.

Ireton, H., & Thwing, E. (1974). *Minnesota Child Development Inventory.* Minneapolis: Behavior Science System.

Jones, R. R. (1985). *The effect of a transition program on low achieving kindergarten students when entering first grade.* Unpublished doctoral dissertation, Northern Arizona University.

Kaufman, A. S., & Kaufman, N. L. (1983). *Kaufman Assessment Battery for Children*. Circle Pines, MN: American Guidance Service, Inc.

Kelley, M. F., & Surbeck, E. (1983). History of preschool assessment. In K. D. Paget & B. A. Bracken (Eds.), *The psychoeducational assessment of preschool children*. New York: Grune and Stratton.

Knoblock, J., Stevens, C., & Malone, M. (1987). *Gesell Developmental Schedules—Revised*. Cleveland: The Psychological Corporation.

Kozol, J. (1990). The new untouchables. *Newsweek*, Winter/Spring, 48–53.

Krechevsky, M. (1991). Project spectrum: An innovative assessment alternative. *Educational Leadership, 49* (6), 43–48.

Krogh, S. (1990). *The integrated early childhood curriculum*. New York: McGraw hill, 1990.

Lichtenstein, R. (1982). *Minneapolis Preschool Screening Instrument*. Minneapolis: Minneapolis Public Schools.

Lowenfeld, V., & Brittain, L. (1975). *Creative and mental growth*. New York: Macmillan.

McCarthy, D. (1972). *McCarthy Scales of Children's Abilities*. Cleveland: The Psychological Corporation.

McCarthy, D. (1980). *The McCarthy Screening Test*. Cleveland: The Psychological Corporation.

Madaus, G. F. (1988). The influence of testing on the curriculum. In L. N. Tanner, (Ed.), *Critical Issues in Curriculum: 87th Yearbook of the National Society for the Study of Education*. Chicago: University of Chicago Press.

Madden, R., Gardner, E., & Collins, C. (1984). *Stanford Early School Achievement Test*. Cleveland: The Psychological Corporation.

Maness, B. J. (1992). Assessment in early childhood education. *Kappa Delta Pi Record, 28* (3), 77–79.

Mardell-Czudnowski, D. D., & Goldenberg, D. S. (1983). *Developmental Indicators for Assessment of Learning (Revised)*. Childcraft Education Corporation.

Markman, E. (1977). Realizing that you don't understand: A preliminary investigation. *Child Development, 48*, 286–292.

Meisels, S. J. (1987). Uses and abuses of developmental screening and school readiness testing. *Young Children, 42* (4–6), 68–73.

Meisels, S. J. (1989a). High stakes testing in kindergarten. *Educational Leadership, 46* (7), 16–22.

Meisels, S. J. (1989b). *Developmental screening in early childhood: A guide*. Washington, DC: National Association for the Education of Young Children.

Meisels, S. J. (1992). Doing harm by doing good: Iatrogenic effects of early childhood enrollment and promotion policies. *Early Childhood Research Quarterly, 7,* 155–174.

Meisels, S. J., & Steele, D. M. (1991). *Early Childhood Developmental Checklist* (Field Trial Edition). Ann Arbor, MI: University of Michigan.

Meisels, S. J., & Wiske, M. S. (1983). *Early Screening Inventory.* New York: Teachers College Press.

Meisels, S. J., Wiske, M. S., & Tivnan, T. (1984). Predicting school performance with the Early Screening Inventory. *Psychology in the schools, 21,* 25–33.

Mills, R. (1989). Portfolios capture rich array of student performance. *The School Administrator, 47* (10), 8–11.

National Association for the Education of Young Children (1985). *National academy of early childhood programs.* Washington, DC: Author

National Association for the Education of Young Children (1988a). Position statement on standardized testing of young children three through eight years of age. *Young Children, 43,* 42–47.

National Association for the Education of Young Children (1988b). *Testing of young children: Concerns and cautions.* Washington, DC: Author

National Association of State Boards of Education (1988). *Right from the start: The report of the National Association of State Boards of Education on early childhood education.* Alexandria, VA: Author

Newborg, J., Stock, J., Wnek, L., Guidubaldi, J., & Sninicki, J. (1984). *The Battelle Developmental Inventory.* DLM Teaching Resources.

Nicholls, J. (1978). The development of the concept of effort and ability, perceptions of academic attainment and the understanding difficult tasks require more ability. *Child Development, 49,* 800–814.

Nicholls, J. (1979). Development of perception of own attainment and casual attributions for success and failure in reading. *Journal of Educational Psychology, 71,* 94–99.

Nurss, J., & McGauvran, M. (1976). *The Metropolitan Readiness Test.* New York: The Psychological Corporation.

Paulson, F. L., Paulson, P., & Meyer, C. (1991). What makes a portfolio? *Educational Leadership, 49,* 60–63.

Phillips, J. L. (1975). *The origins of intellect: Piaget's theory.* San Francisco: W.H. Freeman and Company.

Piaget, J. (1925). De quelques formes primitives de de causalité chez l' enfant. *L 'année Psychologique, 26,* 31–71.

Piaget, J. (1963). *The origins of intelligence in children.* New York: Norton Library.

Royce, J. M., Murray, H. W., Lazar, I., & Darlington, R. B. (1982). Methods of evaluating program outcomes. In B. Spodek (Ed.),

Handbook of research in early childhood education. New York: Free Press.

Scarr, S. (1976). An evolutionary perspective on infant intelligence. Species patterns and individual variations. In M. Lewis (Ed.), *Origins of intelligence: Infancy and early childhood.* New York: Plenum Press.

Schorr, L., & Schorr, D. (1988). *Within our reach: Breaking the cycle of poverty.* New York: Doubleday.

Schweinhart, L. J. (1988). *A school administrator's guide to early childhood programs.* Ypsilanti, MI: High/Scope Press.

Shanklin, N., & Conrad, L. (1991). *Portfolios: A new way to assess student growth.* Denver: Colorado Council of the International Reading Association.

Shepard, L. A., & Smith, M. L. (1985). *Boulder Valley kindergarten study: Retention practices and retention effects.* Boulder, CO: Boulder Valley Public Schools.

Shepard, L. A., & Smith, M. L. (1986). Synthesis of research on school readiness and kindergarten retention. *Educational Leadership, 44,* 78–86.

Shepard, L. A., & Smith, M. L. (1987). Effects of kindergarten retention at the end of first grade. *Psychology in the Schools, 24,* 346–357.

Shepard, L. A., & Smith, M. L. (1988). Escalating academic demand in kindergarten: Counterproductive policies. *The Elementary School Journal, 89,* 135–145.

Smith, M. L., & Glass, G. V. (1987). *Research and evaluation in education and the social sciences.* Englewood Cliffs, NJ: Prentice-Hall, Inc.

Sparrow, S., Balla, D., & Cicchetti, D. (1984). *Vineland Social Maturity Scale.* Circle Pines, MN: American Guidance Services.

Stipek, D. J. (1981). Children's perceptions of their own and their classmates' ability. *Journal of Educational Psychology, 73,* 404–410.

Thorndike, R. L., Hagen, E. P., & Sattler, J. M. (1986). *Stanford-Binet Intelligence Scale—Fourth Edition.* Riverside, CA: Riverside Publishing Co.

Tierney, R. J., Carter, M., & Desai, L. (1991). *Portfolio assessment in the reading-writing classroom.* Norwood, MA: Christopher-Gordon Publishers.

Tyack, D., & Ingram, D. (1977). Children's production and comprehension of questions. *Journal of Child Language, 4,* 211–224.

U.S. Department of Health and Human Services (1979). *Head Start program performance standards self-assessment/validation instrument.* Washington, DC: Administration for Children, Youth and Families.

Uphoff, J., & Gilmore, J. E. (1986). *Summer children: Ready or not for school.* Middletown, OH: J & J Publishing.

Vasta, R. (1979). *Studying children*. San Francisco: Freeman Publishing Company.

Vavrus, L. (1990). Put portfolios to the test. *Instructor* (August), 48–51.

Vermont Department of Education (1988). *Working together to show results: An approach to school accountability for Vermont*. Montpelier, VT: Author.

Vermont Department of Education (1989). *Vermont writing assessment: The portfolio*. Montpelier, VT: Author.

Wechsler, D. (1989). *Wechsler Preschool and Primary Scale of Intelligence—Revised*. New York: The Psychological Corporation.

Wiske, M. S., Meisels, S. J., & Tivnan, T. (1981). The Early Screening Inventory: A study of early childhood developmental screening. In N. J. Anastasiow, W. K. Frankenburg, & A. Fandel (Eds.), *Identification of high risk children*. Baltimore: University Park Press.

Wolf, J. M., & Kessler, A. L. (1986). *Entrance to kindergarten: What is the best age?* Arlington, VA: Educational Research Service.

Wortham, S. C. (1990) *Tests and measurement in early childhood education*. Columbus, OH: Merrill Publishing Company.

Worthen, B. R., & Spandel, V. (1991). Putting the standardized test debate in perspective. *Educational Leadership, 49*, 65–69.

Zagorski, S. (1991). *Beyond standardized testing: An alternative assessment design for young children*. Unpublished manuscript. Milwaukee: University of Wisconsin-Milwaukee.

INDEX

ABOUT THE AUTHOR

DOMINIC F. GULLO is Professor and Program Chair of Early Childhood Education at the University of Wisconsin–Milwaukee. He received his doctorate from Indiana University in the Interdisciplinary Doctoral Program on Young Children. Before becoming a professor, Dom taught for 5 years in the public schools at the kindergarten and prekindergarten levels. He also was a teacher in the Head Start Program. At the university, he teaches courses in curriculum at the prekindergarten and kindergarten levels, and early childhood research. Dom is the father of two sons, Matt and Tim, whose growth and development provided him with many opportunities to fashion his ideas about assessment and evaluation.